NOMOS
GLASHÜTTE

In support of

MÉDECINS SANS FRONTIÈRES
DOCTORS WITHOUT BORDERS

Time for life—with limited edition timepieces in support of Doctors Without Borders/ Médecins Sans Frontières. Each watch raises 100 USD, GBP, or EUR for the Nobel Peace Prize winning humanitarian organization. And still these handcrafted mechanical watches with the red 12 cost the same as the classic models from NOMOS Glashütte. Help now, wear forever.

Funds raised are donated to Médecins Sans Frontières USA, UK, or Germany, depending on the specific model purchased. For MSF UK, the registered charity no. is 1026588. Available at selected retailers in the three participating countries, as well as online. Find your nearest NOMOS retailer at **nomos-watches.com** or order online at **nomos-store.com**

GRANTA

12 Addison Avenue, London WII 4QR | email editorial@granta.com
To subscribe go to granta.com, or call 020 8955 7011 (free phone 0500 004 033)
in the United Kingdom, 845-267-3031 (toll-free 866-438-6150) in the United States

ISSUE 134: WINTER 2016

This selection copyright © 2016 Granta Publications.

Granta, ISSN 173231, is published four times a year by Granta Publications, 12 Addison Avenue, London WII 4QR, United Kingdom.

The US annual subscription price is $48. Airfreight and mailing in the USA by agent named Air Business Ltd, c/o Worldnet-Shipping USA Inc., 156–15 146th Avenue, 2nd Floor, Jamaica, NY 11434, USA. Periodicals postage paid at Jamaica, NY 11431.

US Postmaster: Send address changes to *Granta*, Air Business Ltd, c/o Worldnet-Shipping USA Inc., 156–15 146th Avenue, 2nd Floor, Jamaica, NY 11434, USA.

Subscription records are maintained at *Granta*, c/o Abacus e-Media, Chancery Exchange, 10 Furnival Street, London EC4A 1YH.

Air Business Ltd is acting as our mailing agent.

Granta is printed and bound in Italy by Legoprint. This magazine is printed on paper that fulfils the criteria for 'Paper for permanent document' according to ISO 9706 and the American Library Standard ANSI/NIZO Z39.48-1992 and has been certified by the Forest Stewardship Council (FSC). *Granta* is indexed in the American Humanities Index.

ISBN 978-1-905-881-93-2

English National Ballet

BRAND NEW BALLETS FROM
ASZURE BARTON
ANNABELLE LOPEZ OCHOA
YABIN WANG

SHE SAID

13 – 16 APRIL 2016

ballet.org.uk/shesaid

Supported by the Esmée Fairbairn Foundation,
The Foyle Foundation, the She Said Production
Syndicate, Cockayne – Grants for the Arts
and The London Community Foundation.
English National Ballet is an Associate
Company of Sadler's Wells.

Supported using public funding by
**ARTS COUNCIL
ENGLAND**
LOTTERY FUNDED
Registered Charity 214005

Dancer: Jeanette Kakareka
Photography © Perry Curties
Art Direction and Design:
Charlotte Wilkinson Studio

Sadler's Wells Theatre
sadlerswells.com
0844 412 4300
⊖ Angel

**SADL
ERSW
ELLS**

COMING SOON
THE WENDE MOVES TO ITS NEW HOME

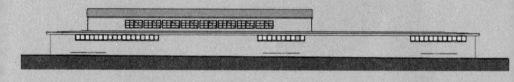

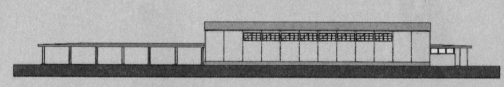

ARCHITECTURAL RENDERINGS
OF THE NEW ARMORY CAMPUS

ROYAL

2016 AT THE ROYAL COURT THEATRE

21 Jan – 12 Mar
Escaped Alone
By Caryl Churchill

22 Jan – 13 Feb
YEN
By Anna Jordan
Royal Court Theatre and Royal Exchange Theatre

International Playwrights: A Genesis Foundation Project
25 Feb – 26 Mar
I See You
By Mongiwekhaya
Royal Court Theatre and Market Theatre Johannesburg

30 Mar – 7 May
X
By Alistair McDowall

5 Apr – 7 May
Cyprus Avenue
By David Ireland
Royal Court Theatre and the Abbey Theatre

17 May – 21 May
Ophelias Zimmer
Directed by Katie Mitchell
Designed by Chloe Lamford
Text by Alice Birch
In association with Schaubühne Berlin

royalcourttheatre.com

Innovation partner

 Coutts

 ARTS COUNCIL ENGLAND
Supported using public funding by

Genesis FOUNDATION

Cyprus Avenue is supported by Cockayne Grants for the Arts,
a donor advised fund of London Community Foundation

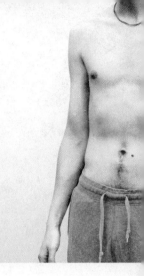

SHE PROTESTIER ZUVIEL.
SHE DOTH PROTEST TOO MUCH

COURT

ARVON

Residential writing c[o]
taught by leading au[thors]

MARK HADDON

DAVID QUANTICK

MONA ARSHI

NADIFA MOHAMED

SUNJEEV SAHOTA

home to your imagination

"One of the most creative and enjoyable experiences I have ever had. I have never learnt so much in such a short time."

KEI MILLER

LOTTERY FUNDED

Supported using public funding by
ARTS COUNCIL ENGLAND

Grants available

arv[on]

PRAIRIE SCHOONER

BOOK
prize
series

2015 Winners

NO CONFESSION, NO MASS

When Are You Coming Home?

[STORIES]

Bryn Chancellor

CONTENTS

Introduction

Wikipedia, that great source of instant human knowledge, tells me that the concept of 'no man's land' was used in the Domesday Book to describe the parcels of land just outside the London city walls. There were later usages – to do with land disputes, with executions, and with some other marginal spaces and activities – until the word became attached to an image of the smoky battlefields of the First World War: blackened stumps of trees, fields of mud, eerie silence alternating with thunderous explosions and the rattle of machine guns.

Someone once owned those fields turned into no man's land.

A human rights lawyer in Israel recently told me that the Jewish settlements on Palestinian land depend on the fact that much of the land was state-owned; that the land registry was incomplete in the Ottoman Empire; and that many fields were farmed by tenants, and owned by émigrés, and, later, refugees. The British administration half-heartedly established a formal land registry, but it didn't go far: the colonial bureaucracy dealt mainly with communities and tribal leaders, not individuals. Settlements are built on land that is designated 'Palestinian' but which may lack clear individual ownership: on such anomalies perpetual conflict thrives.

Who owns the battlegrounds of the so-called Islamic State, I wonder, like the land surrounding Raqqa on the river Euphrates, or al-Raqqah, as it became known after the city fell to Ayadh bin Ghanim in AD 639/640? They grew cotton there, I heard. Perhaps they still do.

Who owns those huge swathes of territory once described as 'Iraqi' or 'Syrian', which are now the no man's land of failed states? I write in the aftermath of the Paris terrorist events; of clichéd headlines and, in Britain, disjointed fragments of resolve, originally generated by the propaganda machinery during the Blitz – ideas of 'carrying on', of not 'giving in'. But what can one say, in the face of such catastrophe? These ideas float around in the ether; like radios, we receive them, and broadcast them as our own. Coded and established political positions creak under the pressure of contradictions: there is the French Muslim leader caught between old resentment and new horror; there is the earnest French socialist caught between the imperative to analyse and understand, and the will to wage war.

Does understanding imply forgiveness? If so we may resist understanding. But I also think it's the only way: there is no alternative. To not attempt to understand is to deny the value of intelligence, in every sense, and the value of the Enlightenment. Here are the terrorists: preparing their guns, stitching their suicide vests. Do they speak as they prepare to kill, and die? I want to know what happens in those rooms, and in those conversations.

So many young people are dead: I look at their photographs. Most of them had parents, of course, and siblings. Some had partners, and children. We know them from the news as *the loved ones*; those who are lost.

Denise Riley, the British poet, wrote, after the death of her son, that the words *sorrow, grief* and *mourning* seemed to her 'too familiar, too sepia, and almost decorative, blandly containing'. Perhaps it is a condition of grief that we can no longer express it. Words lose value, along with everything else.

At a dinner party at the house of an American media entrepreneur, with several international journalists present, the conversation about the events suddenly erupts, and it becomes clear that no one knows what to do. The idea that the Americans failed in Iraq battles with the idea that we must do something. 'Boots on the ground' comes up; a grudging idea of a rapprochement with Putin comes up; Iran comes up. I think of Roberto Saviano, the Italian author of *Gomorrah*, who lives with Mafia death threats. I had seen him earlier that day. He imitated for me the postures of Islamic State followers on the web – Kalashnikovs slung over shoulders; the manly pout; the finger pointing to the sky – and the identical postures, with slightly different hand gestures, of the Mafia guys and the Mexican narco guys: young men (and some women) taking pride in their indifference to death. You don't need religion for that.

Those of us who have left our country of origin, or who have immigrant parents, understand how quickly the lives of immigrants can crystallise around the revival of ancient cultural traditions. We tangle and project, in exile; we make it up as we go along. And those cultural traditions become dangerous when they attach themselves to revolutionary ideology, with its heritage of violence; the solidarity of blood brothers, and the dehumanisation of others. The memes mutate, and reproduce.

But we know this story, too: the aftermath of revolution. The disillusion. Love and affirmation revealed as bullying and brainwashing. Stories of sexual exploitation and drugs. The internal violence, the underhanded ambitions, the informants, the submission, the sly vanity.

A Maoist old man, a cult leader, has just been accused of rape and slavery in a British courtroom. The revolution eats its children, in so many different ways.

Our cover image, by photographer Lorenzo Meloni, is of Kobane, the Syrian town near the Turkish border that was occupied by the Islamic State in the autumn of 2014. Kurdish forces took back the city in January 2015; Kobane was almost destroyed in successive battles. We chose this image because there was hope, somehow, in that motorbike, and that sun, rising or setting. Hope against hope, perhaps, but still. Life carries on. ∎

Sigrid Rausing

from *White Butterflies of Night*

It feels like it was only yesterday morning that I got up from my desk
leaving my biography half-written and half-read
I don't remember whether I believed that I could just
abandon one life to begin another
or whether it was simply a moment of half-consciousness
and returning half a century later proved just as hard
almost like dying and being born again
but the first life had carried on as usual all on its own
without me without my knowledge or desire
what was left on the desk were the contours of my former self
everything to which I'd grown accustomed is now null and void
my biography my views my desk my bed
and no longer did anyone know or remember what ink was
or what an inkwell was or good or bad
what the presence of happiness meant or the meaning of present
while the past and the future had long ceased to exist

Translated from the Russian by Boris Dralyuk

Donetsk airport, March 2015.

PROPAGANDALANDS

Peter Pomerantsev

1

Of all the things Tetyana thought she might become, a soldier was never one of them. Yet here she was. Not a regular soldier, more like some sort of general, someone able to command life and death. Sitting in her father's apartment, in her pyjamas, with her hand over a keyboard, knowing that if she pressed one key she might send many very real people to a very real death, and if she pressed another the revolution and all that she, her friends and thousands of others had fought for might be lost.

Tetyana ran the Facebook page of Hromadske Sektor (the Civic Sector), one of the main opposing groups in the Ukrainian revolution against President Yanukovich and his backers in the Kremlin. It was her job to propagate the idea of positive, peaceful change: videos of a protester playing a piano out on the street when facing a row of riot police; pics of protesters holding mirrors up to the security forces; a drawing of a cop duelling with a protester with the cop holding a gun and the protester 'shooting' with a Facebook sign. Yanukovich controlled the old media but online activists could organise everything from medical help to legal aid, coordinating million-strong protests and raising funds from Ukrainians abroad for food and shelter.

Tetyana had kept up the click-beat over many months of protests. Hromadske Sektor had 45,000 followers and 150,000 visitors attended their events: people who didn't trust politicians but believed in civic leaders and volunteers like Tetyana. She had joined Hromadske because she wanted to be part of a historical moment: something to tell her future children about. But it was just a part-time thing. She would post on the site as she filed stories for her real job as a financial journalist. She told herself she would somehow stay above the fray; she was for democracy and human rights, sure, but she wouldn't get dragged into disinformation; wouldn't get her hands dirty.

Tetyana's shift was in the morning. She was usually based in Kiev but today she happened to be in her home town of Luhansk, one of the capitals in the far east of the country known as the Donbas, where most people watched state or Russian TV, which portrayed the revolution – referred to as the 'Maidan', its name taken from the square where protesters gathered – as a neo-fascist, US-orchestrated conspiracy. Out here, Tetyana never mentioned her work for Hromadske Sektor.

She had woken at 9 a.m. and switched the computer to the live feed coming from the Maidan. At first she thought she had tuned into some action movie by mistake – snipers were mowing people down, and there was blood on the streets. Then her phone rang: activists at the Maidan, relaying messages from the Hromadske Sektor leaders. She could hear guns going off behind them and after a small time-lapse heard them crackle on the live stream too.

'Get people to come to Maidan. We need everyone here.'

But Tetyana could also see posts popping up on her Facebook feed from people on the square warning everyone to flee and save themselves. The activists kept calling her, demanding she tell her followers to come.

'But there are people being killed,' she said.

'The snipers will stop shooting if more people come.'

'And what if they don't?'

'It's your decision.'

It wasn't the first time she'd found her journalistic instinct to remain above the fray clashing with her revolutionary loyalties. A few weeks previously, the pagan-nationalist, balaclava-clad Pravy Sektor (the Right Sector) had started hurling burning Molotov cocktails through the snowstorms at the riot police. Few people had heard of Pravy Sektor until then. There were only a few hundred of them, but all the publicity around their violence had increased their e-profile wildly. Kids looking for a little ultra-violence were now signing up to join them.

Tetyana didn't approve of Pravy Sektor's violence or ideology. The Maidan was full of different 'sectors', including neo-Cossacks and neo-fascists, all able to organise with the help of the Internet. The different sectors had nothing much in common, but it didn't seem right to attack people who were beaten up by the same riot police who beat you up.

Hromadske Sektor decided to ignore Pravy Sektor's violence, but Tetyana couldn't ignore the massacre on Maidan Square that morning. What was her role? Was she, ultimately, a propagandist? A journalist? Was she reporting on the war, or was she a soldier in it? Every time you post or tweet, or just repost or retweet, you become a little propaganda machine. In this new information flux, everyone has to find their own boundaries. Tetyana had reached hers. She refused to encourage crowds to come to the Maidan. She simply reported on what was going on and let people make up their own minds.

Various Hromadske Sektor leaders logged on themselves and urged crowds to come to the Maidan. One hundred and three protesters died in those few days. But the crowds didn't stop coming and the revolution was successful. President Yanukovich fled to Russia, and Hromadske Sektor leaders joined political parties and stood for election. Tetyana didn't want to be involved in party politics and left the movement altogether.

Then the Kremlin began exacting its revenge: Russian TV filled up with invented stories about how Pravy Sektor was coming to slaughter ethnic Russians in Crimea, where most of the population are ethnic Russians. In Sevastopol, the Crimean capital, Cossack groups, separatist parties and Orthodox priests (all funded by the

Kremlin) led crowds begging Putin to rescue them. He obliged and annexed the peninsula.

Russian TV broadcast scare stories about Pravy Sektor coming to murder Russians in East Ukraine, too. The Internet, the medium through which the revolution had been empowered, was flooded with Kremlin content pumped out of 'troll factories' in Russian suburbs. Students were paid a few hundred dollars a day to post pictures, comments and videos, sowing confusion, enmity and panic. The Supreme Allied Commander of NATO called it the greatest information blitzkrieg in history.

In Severodonetsk, Babar Aliev woke to find fifty new Twitter trolls on his tail. Severodonetsk is in East Ukraine, just a few kilometres from the border where Russian troops were massing. A rumour had swept through Severodonetsk's Internet forums about how Pravy Sektor were on their way to haul down the town's Lenin statue, a symbol of their pro-Russian leanings. A motley crew of pro-Russian local groups – Cossacks and wrestlers, fans of laser tag and literary clubs – gathered to defend it. The rumour was false. Someone was just trying to get the pro-Russians fired up.

That wouldn't be hard. Severodonetsk is not a town that feels much historic loyalty to the Ukrainian state. It was built up in the 1950s and 60s: a perfect grid of Soviet blocks of flats, modernist white rectangles designed around a number of science colleges and chemical plants. Like much of Eastern Ukraine, the inhabitants came from across the USSR. After the Second World War, it was one of the few places in the Soviet Union you could go with no papers, a bureaucratic gimmick to gain a new workforce for the heavy industry in the area. When the Soviet Union collapsed, the town slowly went to pot: the factories closed and were stripped of anything valuable, the neat modernist blocks of flats cracked and peeled. Now, the mix of symmetry and dilapidation gives the town the air of an abandoned experiment; people like lab rats, left to eat each other. For many, Russia seems a better place.

Babar (father Azeri, mother Siberian) noticed that the pro-Russian clubs had started to proliferate in 2012, just as Vladimir Putin was facing mass protests against his rule in Moscow. When the Maidan protests began, more clubs appeared. At the time he had thought nothing of it – Ukraine was a democracy after all. Now, he suspected someone had been planning something for a while. During the day the pro-Russians would gather on the main square, where Orthodox priests from the Moscow patriarchate and Communist Party leaders were holding daily rallies calling for unification with Russia, claiming that the Maidan was led by fascists and fed by drugs.

Babar had been in Kiev during the Maidan. He felt that the revolution was a historical leap forward, and was disgusted when he saw the riot police beating up students. He had seen how Yanukovich's party was raiding businesses and pillaging the country: this was a government run as a protection racket, propped up by Putin. And Babar knew about rackets. As a teen in the mid-1990s he had been a gang leader. His speciality was planning and executing complex burglaries. Then he moved on to stripping the local chemical plants of precious metals – gold and platinum (he read up on the periodic table). He dropped the thug life after he was finally caught (he had studied law, and knew how to bribe his way out). But even now, long after establishing himself as a web designer and minor Internet -PR guy, he had the swagger, the shell suits and the fast eyes of the smart hoodlum, as well as the sudden, ecstatic grin of a toddler. In Severodonetsk many still found it hard to believe that Babar had, as he liked to put it, 'developed an aversion to slicing'.

During his time on the Maidan, Babar had developed a Facebook following among pro-Ukrainians in Severodonetsk. Now he used it to fight back against the separatists online, to 'nightmare them' as the Russian phrase goes. Babar put out a story that separatists had beaten up some gay activists and that a battalion of gay fascists was coming from Holland to take revenge. The story was ridiculous but some of the separatists fell for it, which made them look like idiots. Babar also put out a story that two hundred Pravy Sektor agents had holed up in flats in Severodonetsk; that they recorded the names of taxi drivers who wanted Severodonetsk annexed by Russia; that they rode the trams listening to people's conversations; that when they heard pro-separatist talk the agents would take people off the trams and disappear them. The separatists' portals were in a panic and Babar felt he was winning the disinformation war. He wanted the separatists to doubt everything and lose their bearings – he wanted to do to them what the Kremlin was doing to Ukraine.

He also tried to bring a pro-Ukrainian coalition to the streets. But how would he motivate people when there was no overall idea of Ukraine that they related to, and when each tribe in the city lived in its own little information bubble? Babar went to his old friends, the organised-crime bosses, known as 'Vor v Zakone' (thieves in law), who lived according to the strict prison code. Some of them had been in Babar's first gang before he went straight. 'How can you be on the same side as the cops?' he asked them, slipping into Fenya, the old prison jargon which Vor v Zakone still communicate in. 'You used to be an "honest prisoner" (someone who lives by the prison code), now you're a "goat" (a turncoat, the lowest of the low).'

But ultimately it was about money: Babar helped the gangs count the costs to their business interests if the Kremlin invaded. They decided to back Ukraine, and offered him men and guns. So did the hoods who ran the protection rackets, after he made them see where their interests lay. Did they really want to have Russian gangsters on their territory? And while the local gangs had the Ukrainian police in their pocket, the Russian police might have other ideas.

Then Babar went to the businessmen. 'You guys have been to Europe,' he said. 'You know how much easier it is to do business there; no hassle from bureaucrats wanting bribes or gangs wanting protection money. Well, the Maidan is all about us having European rules. Don't you want that?' The businessmen came to his side too.

Now that he had his coalition, Babar reached out to Maidan activists with connections to the new government for backup. Just a few special forces would be enough, he thought. In the spring of

2014, town after town in the east was being taken by separatists backed by Russian special forces, raising the flag of the independent Donetsk and Luhansk People's Republics. Babar waited for a sign from Kiev but none came. He began to suspect the Donbas had been traded in – Moscow would get East Ukraine in return for money and peace. In April the separatists took power in Severodonetsk. The local administration welcomed them, took down the Ukrainian flag and replaced it with the tricolour of the Luhansk People's Republic. The thing that hurt Babar the most was that when the separatists came for him they sent only three men. When he had been arrested back in the 1990s the cops had sent three vans with SWAT teams wearing flak jackets. Now there were just three guys with guns, who put him on a train to Kiev.

By July the Ukrainians had rebooted their decrepit army, now reinforced by volunteer battalions, including the ever-increasing Pravy Sektor. The Ukrainian army surrounded Severodonetsk and lobbed it with heavy artillery. The separatists pulled back to the heartlands of their new republics, the areas around the towns of Donetsk and Luhansk.

Babar returned, but he felt little sense of victory. I met up with him at a Severodonetsk restaurant that was blaring the hi-hat beats of a Russian girl band. The same politicians and cops who had backed the separatists were still running the town, he told me. He complained about the Ukrainian soldiers and volunteer battalions, some of whom had alienated the locals – there had been a shooting during a bar brawl. Worse, one of the volunteer battalions had decided to enforce their authority over one of the local mafias by forcing a gangster to swim across the river. They shot him in the head when he was halfway there. This, Babar felt, wasn't the way to build coalitions.

'The worst thing about all of this,' he told me, 'is that I have to carry a weapon again. Ten years ago I promised never to carry a gun. But I regretted that promise when the separatists came. Next time I will be ready.'

I asked what his plans were for the future. His website business had crashed in the war. He wanted, he said, to create media literacy classes that would help local people distinguish information from disinformation online.

Hadn't he used disinformation himself when he 'nightmared' the separatists with his fake rumours? How did he square that with promoting media literacy campaigns?

'I believe in disinformation for the other side and media literacy for my side,' smiled Babar.

2

'RU still alive you separatist? I wonder how long for?' said the SMS on Andrey Shtahl's mobile. 'As always, there's no number to trace it back to,' said Andrey. He seemed to be used to receiving this kind of message and was more worried that the pro-Ukrainian activists in his home town of Kramatorsk had given out an old address when they had put him on a list of 'traitors': 'What if they go round and beat up the person living there now – someone completely unrelated to any of this?'

Andrey works at the Kramatorsk municipal gazette. When the separatists took Kramatorsk and announced it part of the Donetsk People's Republic, most of the staff fled, but Andrey stayed, taking on the post of editor. His paper published information about sewers and roadworks and schools, and he never strayed into anything political. This saved him when the Ukrainian army took back the town. He was arrested by a pro-Ukrainian volunteer battalion and taken to Dnepropetrovsk. They beat him and held him for three days with a bag over his head, but eventually he was released.

It's Andrey's poetry, rather than his journalism, that has him in trouble with the pro-Ukrainian activists. 'In poetry I can be myself. The head of the Donetsk People's Republic likes my poetry, and responds with improvised verses on Facebook.'

We walked across Kramatorsk's tidy city park and down a grand, neoclassical Soviet avenue to a local cafe with Wi-Fi so we could look up his poetry. In the distance you could see the sun shining off the hills of the Donbas.

There were dozens of pages of Andrey's verses on local poetry forums. We clicked through to his most recent work. It started with satires about the Maidan, done in the style of a Soviet children's poem.

> They will create hell here and horrid night,
> And turn you, my hero, into a sodomite.

'I was against the Maidan,' Andrey tells me. 'I sensed straight away that it would lead to war. I can see the future sometimes.' He had grown up with the young men who joined the separatist forces in Kramatorsk. In his poetry he conveys the careless, chaotic way they decided to take up arms and seize power. 'They were local druggies and gangsters, the kids of policemen and officials. How could I hate them? No one hears the Donbas.'

No one hears the Donbas. I heard that phrase often in the east, a catchphrase expressing the sense that politicians in Kiev didn't understand local needs. As the conflict spread eastwards, Andrey's poetry became more grim:

> I used to be a musician and artist,
> But now I woke up as a separatist . . .
> I live in Rus, Rus isn't dead yet!
> What I wish for is a bullet in the Prime Minister's head!

Much of the poetry evokes Soviet motifs and songs. Andrey is haunted by a memory from his teens, when he was on a school trip to Lithuania in 1991 and witnessed the crowds trying to pull down a statue of Lenin. On the long train journey back to Donetsk he wrote his first poem, an allegory of the Soviet Union as a train that has become too old, and of a country falling into civil war.

'Lenins were falling then and they are falling again now,' he sighs. 'Back then I already had a bad feeling about the future.'

When we met in Kramatorsk the government in Kiev had just passed a set of laws forbidding Soviet street names and symbols. The Lenin statue on the central square had already been pulled down, leaving an empty plinth with a Ukrainian flag tacked on. These directives were pushed through by a former leader of the Hromadske Sektor, Volodymyr Viatrovych, and had been condemned as 'vague and potentially authoritarian' by the Organization for Security and Co-operation in Europe. Viatrovych had argued that the laws were part of the information war against the Kremlin and its non-stop diet of Soviet movies and social-media campaigns that reframe the present as perpetual war against eternally returning fascists. But if anything, these anti-Soviet laws played into the hands of the Kremlin, shifting the political discourse of the Maidan from the future to the past.

'The communists built everything here. Anyone who ever achieved anything was from the party – why should we forget them?' said Andrey. 'There are a lot of people here who can't talk openly about what they think. They live online instead, and it's important for them not to be lonely. I can understand what they are going through.'

It was online, I noticed, where Andrey's nostalgia was nurtured. The plethora of new media broke up a shared vision of the present, but kindled virtual realities of hallucinated pasts where something whole still seemed possible.

I was denied entry to the Donetsk People's Republic – there was an uptick in shelling during my visit and many foreign journalists were denied visas, but in Kramatorsk I found the former head of information policy in Donetsk, Elena Malyutina. What remained of her ministry-in-exile had set up office in a disused bank in town. Every weekend Elena travelled to see her husband and parents in Donetsk: unlike her, they had pledged their allegiance to the pro-Russian republic, a family split apart by propaganda. She spoke calmly and slowly, like a patient teacher to a child, her large blue eyes looking straight at me and her neatly made-up face nodding as if to check that I understood everything she talked about was quite serious, however absurd it sounded. Many of her sentences started with 'You have to understand . . .'

'You have to understand: when I cross into the DNR [the Donetsk National Republic, another name for the Donetsk People's Republic] it's like going through the looking glass. A parallel reality.' She took out her laptop and opened photos of cheering crowds in the centre of Donetsk, all draped in banners and ribbons with the Ukrainian flag. 'This is at Euro 2012,' explained Elena. 'We organised all the festivities. We followed the model of Soviet parades, something people in Donetsk understood, and grafted Ukrainian motifs onto them.'

But it was hard to connect locals to Ukraine. Kiev had allowed its leaders to run Donetsk as their personal fiefdom. In surveys people described their identity as 'Donbasskij' or 'Soviet'. To the south Donetsk had the sea and to the north it had forests: it was a self-contained zone. If locals travelled anywhere it was to Russia, though many wouldn't even register that they were crossing into a different country: borders were loose here, state borders as much as those between past and present.

'Deep down many people hated Ukraine,' says Elena. 'My husband was one of them.'

The Maidan was an affront to Donetsk male pride. Kiev had stood up to a president from Donetsk while Donetsk, whose people knew Yanukovich's corruption better than anyone, had always put up with him. When separatists and Russian special forces took over government buildings and announced a referendum calling for independence, her husband and parents voted for it, while Elena and her teenage daughter voted against.

'You're a lawyer,' she said to her husband. 'You must realise you can't build anything on blood. You need evolution.'

'Evolution hasn't worked for us. We're going to build a new republic,' he responded.

The new republic closed down access to Ukrainian media. Now there was just Russian TV and the new DPR channel, which used all the language of Sovietica and the Second World War: 'We will liberate our villages from the fascists'; 'The fascists won't pass!' There were Soviet-style military parades and Soviet-style pioneer groups; Soviet-style sports festivals and calls to 'live like our ancestors', to 'protect our roots' and 'honour our grandparents'. 'Everything will be like it once was,' people said. Quotes from the leaders of the Donetsk People's Republic read like posters of Lenin in Soviet times.

Meanwhile, the Ukrainian army had advanced and was shelling Donetsk and the surrounding cities. The DPR had promised a return to the USSR and now it was being shelled with Soviet-era weapons. Civilians, including children, were killed. Russian and DPR TV didn't need to invent horror stories any more as they could now show authentic footage of dead children.

'The enemy's cry of "Ukraine above all else" clearly shows they want to destroy anything Russian,' said the leaflets handed out on the street. 'They always wanted to kill us.'

'Kiev wants to drag us into the EU and destroy our Orthodox churches. It means we will end up poor. And those who put us in concentration camps will become richer. The US wants to take our shale gas and disgrace our holy places.'

It made no sense, but that almost seemed to be the point: break down critical thinking with absurdities and false logic, then open people up emotionally with images of suffering and trauma before promising them glory. Russian and DPR propaganda was working on the same psychological principles as that of many sects.

'I want to go back to my motherland,' said Elena's best friend, a PR manager at Donetsk's premier international hotel.

'Which motherland?' asked Elena.

'The USSR.'

'But can't you tell this is not real?'

Her friend looked at her with glazed eyes.

Elena's husband could see that gangsters were taking over the town, but he still thought separation from Ukraine was the way forward. When Elena pointed out that there were Russian secret service guys everywhere, he refused to recognise their presence. Her daughter was cracking, too: 'It's hard to be a Ukrainian patriot when your own side is bombing you.'

Every day the Donetsk People's Republic project was getting darker. Pro-Ukrainian prisoners of war were interrogated on camera at knifepoint. They were made to eat their Ukrainian badges. They were marched down the streets to show that resistance was useless. The footage was put online by the perpetrators with the aim of intimidating any opposition. In the town of Slovyansk, run by the (allegedly retired) Russian FSB agent Igor Girkin, Stalin-era martial law was imposed. Girkin was a re-enactor of historical battles, who would express his fantasies in online communities of Stalinists and Tsarists, where nostalgists yearned for a return to Soviet order and empire grandeur: now he was making them real. When Slovyansk was retaken by Ukraine, human rights groups and journalists found that firing squads had executed people for petty theft and bundled them into mass graves.

Elena decided she needed to get herself and her daughter out. They left for Kramatorsk where most of her ministry had fled. I wondered how deep she thought the cult of nostalgia really went in her home town.

'It's partly a masquerade. Many people play along. Among my old colleagues maybe 70 per cent left but 30 per cent had to stay because they simply couldn't find work anywhere else.'

For all the rhetorical passion of people like Andrey Shtahl, when the Lenins are brought down in East Ukraine, most of the time there are hardly any protests. Few actually care. The nostalgia turns out to be yet another hologram.

'If there was no TV for a few weeks the DPR would fade,' said Elena. In Kramatorsk she is setting up a regional TV channel which will avoid the Kremlin's favourite playing fields of history and ideology and focus on people's daily lives: roads and food prices. She wants to bring Donetsk back to reality.

3

I was in Kharkiv, crossing Europe's second-largest square in Ukraine's second-largest city, on my way to visit a refugee camp for those fleeing the shelling from the front lines of the Donbas. The light was golden, giving a Hollywood glaze to the Soviet neoclassical government buildings on the square, relics of Kharkiv's seventeen years as Ukraine's capital between 1917 and 1935. The memory of that lost status permeates this town, with TV shows and websites dedicated to recalling the 'second capital'. It is this yearning that Yanukovich's old party and the Kremlin tried to play on when, right after the Maidan, they attempted first to make Kharkiv the capital of a breakaway pro-Russian Ukraine, and then turn it into a new separatist city republic. There had been both pro-Maidan and anti-Maidan crowds on Freedom Square: 30 per cent of the people in Kharkiv define themselves as Russian, almost 70 per cent as Ukrainian. As the Russian army massed on the border a few kilometres away the anti-Maidan group swelled with busloads of Russian 'tourists' (you could see the Russian licence plates on the coaches). The anti-Maidan crowds dragged the pro-Maidan supporters across the square by the hair, kicking, taunting and spitting at them. One of the 'tourists' climbed the spire of the town hall and planted a Russian flag on it.

Unlike what they did in Severodonetsk, Kiev acted forcefully in Kharkiv, sending special forces to arrest the pro-Russian activists. Billboards went up, threatening people with a visit from the secret services for 'Everyday Separatism' (no one was quite sure what that meant). Menacing leaflets were handed out predicting problems for anyone who advocated joining Russia (no one was quite sure who was behind the leaflets). At the same time bombs kept going off at bars where pro-Ukrainians liked to meet. Three people were killed by a bomb placed in a bin at a pro-Ukrainian march.

The morning I arrived, the local Pravy Sektor threw stones at the office of the old Yanukovich party, whose leaders were trying to make a political comeback. Shots were fired. But the physical violence, I soon realised, was orchestrated. The Ukrainian side had come prepared with cameras to show their online supporters they had muscle, but they also filmed the events in such a way that it made it seem like they had been shot at first.

The pro-Russian side, on the other hand, had tried to provoke an attack. Toughs were bussed in from the suburbs to taunt the pro-Ukrainians. All of this was edited out of the evening news on the main TV channel: it looked like the Russians were victims of unprovoked pro-Ukrainian aggression. The channel belonged to the mayor, a former gangster turned billionaire known as Gepa – a member of Yanukovich's party. At the start of the Maidan he had first backed the Russian side, then fled to Moscow (he later claimed he had been in Switzerland), then returned as a Ukrainian patriot playing all sides. After the evening news came a public service ad which showed beatific shots of Kharkiv. The screen suddenly went black: 'Our peaceful city is under threat from terrorism,' went the voice-over. A head in a balaclava appeared representing 'terrorism': it could have been a Pravy Sektor fighter, a separatist or even Pussy Riot. It was unclear what the threat was, all you knew was that it was out there. A news segment about how Satanists had defaced a children's playground followed.

I found the refugee camp on the edge of town. Among tidy German Portakabins by pretty beds of posies and amid the smell of frying onions I talked to a family getting ready for dinner. I asked what news they watched. They told me they had given up believing anyone as both sides lied: the Russians would falsely report their towns had been laid to waste by Ukrainians; the Ukrainians would report great Ukrainian military victories when the separatists had merely retreated. But what emerged from their total scepticism was a sense that, if nothing around them could be trusted, then shadowy powers must be moving their lives: Obama's or the Masons' hidden hands stood behind every bombing.

'Everything has already been decided', they told me, 'up on high.'

Dzerzhinsk is a mining town at the very edge of the territory held by Ukrainian forces: separatist positions are a couple of kilometres away. There was a summer storm brewing when I arrived, thunder mixing with the sound of heavy artillery. A few days earlier a shell had hit the local lake. Fish had flown out onto the cracked paths or floated dead to the surface. The people of Dzerzhinsk ate the fish, but there were still a few drying on the paths and many more were floating belly up in the lake. The smell was strong.

I travelled with a small crew from an Internet-TV station from Kiev, one of the few Ukrainian media organisations not in the pocket of an oligarch. Driving through town, we passed along roads with coffin-sized craters; empty factories with their walls ripped out. A young boy leading his drunk mother down the lanes; local men with scabs on their faces. I stopped to photograph a concrete coal store with a gaping hole in its walls. I assumed it had been shelled but it turned out it had been taken apart long before the war by locals looking for scrap metal.

Dzerzhinsk is named after Felix Dzerzhinsky, the man responsible for the first Soviet secret police, the notorious Cheka. When I asked a local teenage girl whether she knew who he was, she told me she'd 'heard of him at school but couldn't remember'. This wasn't unusual: a few weeks earlier, a TV channel had done a joke report about how young people in Dzerzhinsk had no idea whom the town was named after. Later that year it was renamed Toretsk, in accordance with the laws against Soviet names. There were no great protests.

The mineshafts were dark against the thundery skyline. Some of the mines were now disused. Others were rusty, but functional. The local bureaucrats sold the coal to subsidised electricity plants controlled by other friendly bureaucrats. It's the subsidies that make money, not the sales. The people of Dzerzhinsk are bit players in someone else's scam.

The mayor of Dzerzhinsk has weathered every revolution. In April 2014 he welcomed the separatists with open arms. The two newspapers under his control supported the Donetsk People's Republic. When the Ukrainian army retook the town a few months later, they shelled the town hall. The mayor quickly cut a deal with them. Online videos of the mayor expressing support for the Donetsk People's Republic were deleted, and the online archive of the newspapers was wiped. But though the town was now officially in Ukrainian territory, you still couldn't get Ukrainian TV unless you had a cable package. Russian and DPR TV are still available everywhere – Dzerzhinsk may be in Ukrainian territory, but it is still under the Kremlin's informational sovereignty.

The pro-Ukrainian activists were jumpy. There was Oleg, an older man with a grey moustache and a cap. He had been one of the miners who helped bring down the Soviet Union in the great strike of 1989, blocking the roads with broken glass to stop the Kremlin's tanks. Volodya was younger, with big arms and a boy-band fringe. He was a miner too but had worked in Sweden for several years. He knew things didn't have to be this way. Last week, Oleg, Volodya and the other dozen or so pro-Ukraine activists received army mobilisation orders. When Volodya went for his health check, the nurses blurted out that the activists were all on a list together.

Volodya and Oleg were sure the mayor wanted the activists, with their annoying anti-corruption rallies, out of town. They were worried that he'd bribed Kiev to stay in power. That Kiev was ready to abandon them.

'If there's no mention of us on TV, then it won't be a big deal if the town is lost,' said Volodya. 'We're being erased.' In the front of his van was a stack of leaflets:

7 TO 12 YEARS PUNISHMENT FOR EVERYDAY SEPARATISM: CALL THIS NUMBER IF YOU SPOT AN EVERYDAY SEPARATIST!

HOW TO SPOT AN EVERYDAY SEPARATIST?
— CALLS FOR RUSSIA TO INVADE
— INSULTS UKRAINIAN VALUES
— SPREADS LIES
— PLANTS DEFEATIST FEELINGS

I asked Volodya where he had obtained the leaflets. He told me with no little pride he had made them himself. I asked whether that was such a good idea.

'The telephone numbers on them aren't even real,' he said. 'They're just to intimidate people. We're all alone here. We need to do something.'

We arrived at a Soviet block of flats, rising above an area of wooden shacks, several of which had been blown apart. The Ukrainian army base was five hundred metres away and this area was hit frequently. Oleg showed us the shrapnel holes in the metal door of the apartment block. Some women were on a bench outside the front door. They were angry that the Ukrainians had put their base near here. There had been no fighting when the town had been part of the DPR. The Ukrainian army had brought the war with them. One woman told me how a shell had exploded through her balcony.

Oleg got angry: 'Our mayor is a separatist. That's why the army is here. He should be in prison.'

'I worked all my life for pennies and what's my reward?' said a woman going past in a sunflower-patterned dress: 'Bombs!'

'They came from over there – those are Ukrainian positions! That's not DPR,' shouted one of the women. Later she showed me a crater in the ground. A tree had collapsed into it. 'Look,' she said, 'it's clear it came from the Ukrainian position.'

It didn't seem clear at all. I thought it unlikely the Ukrainians could shell themselves from five hundred metres away. But this wasn't about piecing together evidence. Journalists who had travelled the region had warned me about this phenomenon: people would rearrange the evidence to fit the world view they saw on television, however little sense it made.

'The Ukrainians are bombing each other!' said someone else. 'The Pravy Sektor wants to march on Kiev and they're fighting each other.'

'It's the Americans. They've come here to take our gas. I heard there are wounded American soldiers in the local hospitals.'

Oleg was becoming increasingly irate, shouting at the women that they were traitors. They started shooing him away. He took off his shirt and showed them a bullet wound: he said the Russians had shot at him when he delivered food to the front lines. He said Putin was in Ukraine because he was afraid that Russia would fall apart. The women said Putin wasn't afraid of anything.

Oleg went to the car and came back with the leaflets and started handing them out.

'Ha – you think we're afraid of this?' The women laughed and threw the papers in the bin.

Then they turned to the cameraman and me and started shouting at us.

'You'll re-edit what we say anyway. Why should we trust you? Nobody wants to hear the Donbas!'

That phrase again, repeated here like a mantra: *Nobody hears the Donbas*. It reminded me of a prayer, a religious lamentation for a lost God, the recurring theme of the Psalms crying out to a vanished God; the Yom Kippur prayers that beg God to hear the people.

'O God who answered Abraham, Jacob and Isaac, O God who answered us in Sinai, Hear, Hear, Hear the Donbas!'

I woke up in the billiards room. It was still dark and I nearly collided with some soldiers who were slumped, fully clothed, on sofas. One soldier was sleeping with his head on the floor, propping up his fat torso; he was so exhausted that he didn't notice he was sleeping in a half-headstand. Outside, the rose garden and tennis court were just becoming visible in the dawn light. The roses were wilted and the tennis net was missing. I could hear rhythmic splashing: a soldier was doing breaststroke in the outdoor pool. The light was coming on fast, revealing summer houses and garages; high-security fences; the hills beyond and the dark green, almost black, pine forests of the Luhanschina. We were north-east of Dzerzhinsk, on the edge of the territory held by Ukraine where it bordered the Luhansk People's Republic.

I had tagged along with a friend who ran an Internet-TV channel in Kharkiv: the soldiers, who were from Ukrainian Kharkiv's 92nd Brigade, wanted her to tell the country about their frustrations. They were bivouacked on the country estate of a deposed local minigarch, formerly the head of the Luhansk Court of Appeal. He was now lying low in Kiev, waiting to see which side would win. There was a hyperrealist portrait of his wife in the billiards room: a plump, grinning blonde lying in a summer field with a garland of red poppies over her head.

In a cottage near the pool an officer was making breakfast: chopped cabbage and corned-beef meatballs. He was angry at the government. 'Look at this food: none of it comes from the government, it's all delivered by volunteers.'

The Ukrainian army was fed and equipped by volunteers, many originally from the Maidan. They raised money on Facebook and crowdsourced boots, binoculars and uniforms, including US Army gear contributed by the Ukrainian diaspora – which had led some observers to conclude that American soldiers were fighting in the Donbas.

'If you watched TV you'd think the government cares about us,' complained the officer. 'But Putin treats his army much better.'

Ukrainian TV was bursting with war propaganda. The President, Petro Poroshenko, a billionaire chocolate manufacturer who owns one of the 24-hour news channels, was filmed in military fatigues inspecting well-equipped troops. There were slow-motion clips of proud wives waving soldiers off to war, or meeting them by the train with tears of joy. It was the sort of war propaganda that was used to build national morale and spur mobilisation everywhere throughout the twentieth century: glossing over the failures of logistics, lying about the number of casualties and ignoring civilian deaths.

Russia was not officially at war with Ukraine and the two countries had not broken diplomatic or economic ties. One of the clever twists of the Kremlin's doctrine of twenty-first-century conflict, known as 'hybrid' or 'non-linear' war, is that it allows a country to wage war without ever openly declaring it, while destabilising opponents from within through propaganda and infiltration, stirring civil war.

But business people carried on trading as if nothing was happening. Ukraine was reluctant to declare war first, thus becoming the *de jure* aggressor and imposing economic sanctions few people wanted. This had a knock-on effect on the war propaganda. On the one hand, the conflict in the east was not officially defined as war against Russia. But neither could it be called a war against Eastern Ukraine, since that frame was aligned with the Kremlin's claim that this was a civil war.

Propaganda activists tried to define the war in their own ways online: this was a war against 'Soviet mentality', against the *vatniki* – a pejorative name for anyone who was against the Maidan. But plenty of Ukrainians shared the Soviet mentality, not least the soldiers. Most of the soldiers in the 92nd were professional troops from Kharkiv who had been against the Maidan: their sympathies were with the riot police sent to quell the revolution. The online activists were trying to make up their own propaganda as they went along, but it risked playing into the Kremlin's strategy of divide and rule.

Later, the soldiers took us to the front line. Every vehicle was a different make. I sat in the back of a small Nissan jeep and was told to look out the window to watch for separatist snipers. The window had been shattered in a previous gunfight, and was held together with scotch tape. You couldn't see a single thing through it.

We stopped on the edge of a bluff opposite the separatist positions on the other side of the river. You could just about see them with the naked eye. 'If they start shooting, jump away from the cars,' said the commander, known as the ComBrig. 'They will aim for.'

The ComBrig ordered heavy artillery to spread out along the bluff in a show of strength. Then he timed how long it took the separatists to get their people in position: a ruse to get the other side to reveal where they had hidden their forces on the far side of the bluff. The story was that new Russian units had recently arrived.

From there, we drove to the village of Lobachevo, a collection of single-storey wooden houses at skewed angles. A cow stood on the road, staring at an outhouse. Three elderly men in dusty string vests, flip-flops on dirty feet, sat drinking and smoking on some logs outside. One of them, known as Uncle Kolya, had no teeth. He claimed a separatist had knocked them out after he refused to sing the Luhansk National Republic anthem. The soldiers suspected he had concocted the story just for them, and that the second their back was turned he would curse Ukraine. 'We spent a long time winning their trust,' said the ComBrig. 'At first they thought we were all Pravy Sektor monsters from the Russian propaganda machine.'

Across the riverbank you could see the separatists with rifles slung over their shoulders, pacing up and down by the old ferry station. The ferry had been blown up during the fighting. Families who lived on different sides of the river had been split. The school was on one side, and the shops were on the other. Local women crossed in a tiny rowboat with a tiny motor. They complained that if they carried more than one bag of potatoes they could be done for smuggling contraband. They didn't care about Ukraine, Russia or the Luhansk National Republic. They cared about their village, and their potatoes.

We drove out from Lobachevo, past abandoned churches and blown-up bridges which had collapsed into the green river, past women walking with goats. There was no obvious profit to be made from any of this land. Kiev had done nothing to develop it in twenty years of independence but the Kremlin had little need for it either. If you looked closely, both sides were prepared to lose Luhanschina: the Kremlin wanted to hand it back to Ukraine while maintaining covert political control; Kiev made noises about 'unity' but many people, from top brass to academics, argued that the best outcome was a frozen territory the Kremlin had to fund and feed.

War used to be about capturing territory and planting flags, but something different was at play out here. Moscow needed to create a narrative about how pro-democracy revolutions like the Maidan lead to chaos and civil war. Kiev needed to show that separatism leads to misery. What actually happened on the ground was almost irrelevant – the two governments just needed enough footage to back their respective stories. Propaganda has always accompanied war, usually as a handmaiden to the actual fighting. But the information age means that this equation has been flipped: military operations are now handmaidens to the more important information effect. It would be like a vastly scripted reality TV show if it weren't for the very real deaths: a few months after my visit, on 3 November 2015, the Kharkiv 92nd would be caught up in a firefight by Lobachevo. The ComBrig was wounded, but survived.

Our vehicles stopped by a bend in the river. The soldiers took off their donated uniforms, grabbed a Tarzan swing that drooped from a tree on the bank and leapt into the water, whooping. Some tried backflips and others bellyflopped: this was a daily ritual to help them wind down after the patrol.

The ComBrig was in the river when his phone went off. It was an emergency: shelling had started again over no man's land. The previous day the 92nd had agreed on a ceasefire with the separatists so that electricians could come into the firing zone and fix some cables. Now the separatists were shelling overhead. If the 92nd fired back it would look like they were firing on civilians. 'Whatever you do, don't react,' said the ComBrig, fatigues hurriedly pulled over wet boxer shorts. 'It's a provocation for the cameras.'

In the evening we drank moonshine cognac from a plastic bottle and looked up at the stars, as thick as grapes, listening for the sound of shells and following traces of missiles in the sky. We were looking for signs of our military fate like medieval men had looked at comets in search of meaning. Some of the stars moved around: drones, spying on us. I felt as though I was inside a modern icon: the information war had broken so much of my sense of scale. The activists behind their laptops seemed as big as ministries; mythological fiends from Twitter as real as tanks. The borders between Russia and Ukraine, between past and present, between soldier and civilian, rumour and evidence, actor and audience had buckled, and with that the whole rational, ordered sense of perspective suddenly gave way to a thinking which was magical and mystical, where reality was unknowable and seemed to be decided somewhere up on high by divine conspiracies. The layers of spheres and angels had been replaced with endlessly reflecting media stories, where information was no longer simply the recording of action but the point of it. We were all caught up in the recordings, revolving and refracting in the information heavens.

A drone paused up above us.

'Smile,' said the ComBrig. 'It's taking your photo.' ∎

Friday Afternoon with Boko Haram

I spent the Hezbollah war in Nigeria eating hummus in a Syrian
cafe and watching rockets. Nights alone in a Kano hotel, I saw a
girl grow famous on TV. I almost died in the north, you know.
No you don't. No one does but the photographer who crouched
shotgun and begged the mob with hammered swords for his
camera and passport. Its folio of spent pages, like the ordered laws
of nations, was as irrelevant as our heads would be once cleaved
from our pleading bodies. We'd be flung between them until
someone got bored and tossed us into the soaked dirt. The young
blonde now hosts a special on what to do in Dubai; that obscene
indoor ski slope, jeeps that bounce like jelly donuts over dunes lit
to look friendly. There must be so many of us, spies who are really
academics, checking into obscure hotels, ordering contraband
beer. Hating ourselves, we pick at what swells until the larvae
embedded in our backs hatch through the skin, and moths escape
like subcutaneous angels.

© TEO SENG KEAT
Antic Radio, 2007

BASE LIFE

George Makana Clark

Overhead bullets concuss the air, disrupt Nzinga's world. There's no aim to the gunfire, no malice. A government patrol has stumbled on her father's distant sentries, both sides firing blind in their mutual retreat.

Nzinga has gone into the forest against Mamãe's wishes to listen to Voice of America on a radio that looks like a Coke can. She high-crawls across a small clearing, her unzipped rucksack trailing by a strap looped round the crook of her elbow. The bag contains the radio and a teal-and-blue Caboodles makeup case 'with pink slide-out trays for the girl on the go'. Nzinga finds cover behind a fallen trunk and burrows into the leaf litter. Another fusillade whips through the canopy, and branches snap overhead with sharp clicks like beetles. The firefight signals an end to base life.

Mao's words resonate in the moment, spoken in her mother's voice: *Be resolute. Fear no sacrifice.* Nzinga buries her face in the decayed leaves and racemose orchids, blurring the precise brushstrokes of her mascara.

The skirmish is over as quickly as it begins. The communists will return in force, supported by Cuban commandos. Papa's sentries will withdraw to a prearranged rendezvous point so as not to lead the enemy to the base camp, buying their families time to decamp and mine the approach.

Nzinga raises her head and scans the forest. She sniffs for traces of sweat, gun oil, the harsh detergent the government soldiers use on their fatigues, but there's only rotting vegetation, cloying orchids, her Electric Youth fragrance that is, like the makeup case and radio, a gift from the American soldier, Tee Baptiste.

First Sub-Officer Burgos surveys the ground where the firefight took place. Shells everywhere. No casualties, save for a monkey felled by an errant bullet, its neck broken from the fifteen-meter fall from canopy to forest floor. Burgos lifts the creature by the scruff, its head lolling on its neck. Raindrops bead on its fur.

'See what I tell you?' he says, shaking the small carcass at a patrol of Angolan soldiers. 'Aim short bursts at specific targets!' Burgos has learned that his men's response to hostile fire is to empty clip after clip into the forest, the rapid discharge forcing their rifle barrels upward until they're shooting into the air like children with party poppers, severed vines and mossy canopy ferns falling around them like streamers.

Burgos detests Angola, its damp decay, the way its air hangs on his face like a sour dishrag. He distances himself from the chattering, undisciplined soldiers who cluster together, inviting slaughter, their ragbag of Cuban olive and Portuguese camo fatigues jarring against the forest palette. The civil war has decimated the veteran cadres of the Angolan Armed Forces, leaving only hastily trained boys and criminals to fill the brigades.

Burgos wears the red beret and stinger armband of the Black Wasps, the commando branch of the Revolutionary Army of Cuba, part of an expeditionary force sent to help the government in their struggle against capitalist terrorists backed by CIA thugs and the South African apartheid war machine. For him, the forest floor is a game board: before he advances into a square, he must first scan it for the sharp angle of a pressure fuse, the razor-straightness of a tripwire, the lug-sole imprints of American-made jungle boots worn by the terrorists, or else risk being removed from play.

There's something bright red amid the forest litter. Burgos waves off the soldiers, and they move on, joking loudly, happy to be rid of the Cuban commando. There are no disruptions in the air, metallic clicks, sharp breaks in the insect hum. Burgos approaches, examines the object, a Coca-Cola can. Slowly, he paces out the thirty-meter kill zone of an American-made bounding mine, shoulders his rifle, and fires. The can bounces, but not as high as if it had been empty. Again he approaches, inspects it, marvels.

A transistor radio.

He switches it on. Remarkably it still works, the bullet having passed harmlessly through the paper speaker cone. He recognizes Madonna's voice, singing about boys who make her rainy day; about the material world; about being a material girl, and thumbs back the volume dial until the radio clicks off. The red aluminum is free of water deposits and algae, recently dropped. Who, in this destitute nation, would willingly discard such a luxury?

The Angolan soldiers have melted into the forest, though Burgos can still hear their voices. There's an impression on the ground near the radio, dragged leaves, the humus exposed. Someone crawling, Burgos reckons. What sort of imbecile enters a forest alone in the middle of a civil war? The imprint suggests a person of slight stature, an adolescent maybe. Nothing else is out of place, no planted landmines, at least not recently.

Burgos replaces the radio where he found it and recedes into a stand of yellowwood to wait, unseen, for its owner to return.

When Nzinga returns to camp, the older women are already striking the tents. Children sink jerry cans into the stream. Two oldsters, veterans of the War of Independence against the Portuguese, fuel a five-ton truck, US Army surplus provided by Tee Baptiste. They'll load up the tent floorboards, generators, paraffin stoves and cots and drive east into the interior to resume base life. Papa's soldiers, mostly men, have piled into a dozen steel-plated SUVs and pickups and raced west to harry the advancing communist troops and cover the mobile withdrawal. The women stand perimeter guard, facing the enemy's likely approach, a single dirt track.

Nzinga stands quietly behind her papa while he sits in his folding chair and strokes his pointy beard, a tin cup filled with rain-watered brandy balanced on his knee. She follows his gaze out over the vanishing base camp, beyond the parade ground to the floating bridge constructed of tree trunks set lengthwise over oil drums that leads to a place where there's no need for offensive operations.

Her mother thinks the bridge should be blown up, removing the option of retreat from the table, severing the American supply line and all strings attached thereto. The cadre grows impatient with Papa's strategy of non-engagement. Nzinga knows he retains command only out of respect for his earlier military successes, and through the support of the oldsters. The very fact of the cadre's survival, Papa explains to his soldiers, to his wife, is a threat to the communist government.

Mamãe packs textbooks with such force that she splits the seam of a cardboard box. She is much younger than Papa, darker, untainted by Portuguese blood, hair cropped tight against her skull. She is the camp schoolmistress, her curriculum a grab bag of poetry, capitalist dogma and English, the language of commerce. Mao's political discourse is presented only in a handful of bastardized quotes that, taken together, are meant to represent the sketchy, wrong-headed manifestos of the communists, though every child can recite the chairman's aphorisms on guerrilla warfare: *Despise the enemy, but respect his tactics.*

There's a noise like hands slapping against empty buckets, musical and urgent. Nzinga races toward the rackety sound that grows louder and closer, the unmistakable rumble of Tee Baptiste's Chevy Bonanza lumbering across the floating bridge, its camper shell filled with Portuguese-to-English dictionaries, cylinders of Pringles potato chips, bandoleers and belt-feeds of small- and large-caliber bullets, field rations, comic books and *Teen* magazine, launcher grenades, chocolate-chip pound cakes wrapped in foil sleeves, string-tie headbands and 'Bouncing Betty' bounding mines.

Tee Baptiste steps down from the cab onto the parade ground. His smile stretches past his incisors as a sea of children engulf him with outstretched hands, each wanting to touch a bit of America. He wears a New Orleans Saints ball cap instead of his usual green beret. His faded jungle fatigues are professionally tailored, starched and pressed, master sergeant's chevrons sewn onto the collar, a Special Forces tab arcing across his meaty shoulder. Tee Baptiste is here to train and supply Papa's men in their fight against the Cubans and their puppet government in Angola.

Nzinga stands on the periphery, studying the American, his nonchalance, the practiced way he leans against the Chevy's fender, eyes obscured in the shadow of the ball cap, one foot against the tire. His haircut is non-regulation, the back of his neck hidden beneath tight Jerry curls. Of course he's brought something special just for her.

When the children finally disperse, Tee Baptiste wraps his thick arms around Nzinga, and she feels the centrifugal force as he spins her in a circle, the earth falling away. He sets her down and stretches a thick leg toward her, turning his foot about. His fatigue trousers are bloused into a glossy pair of Givenchy harness boots. He pulls one off and hands it to her. 'Put it on, Home Fry.' It smells like popcorn and polish, the leather hot and damp on her bare foot.

'Does Givenchy make shoes for women?' she asks.

'Yeah they do. Cost you some serious paper, but they rock any outfit.'

Nzinga slides her foot out of the boot and returns it to Tee Baptiste. 'I saw these in *Teen*. Rick Springfield has a pair.'

'Rick may wear the same boots as me, but he never be phat like me.'

Nzinga loves the English language, all the words to describe the same thing, the American slang so different from the stuffy Portuguese poetry her mother teaches, the advertisements lyrical in their brevity. Nzinga has taped a half-page spread from *Teen* magazine inside the lid of her makeup case, a photograph of a green-eyed American girl wearing a pearl bracelet with the caption: PROMISE ROGER YOUR STRAWBERRY KISSES.

Tee Baptiste unsnaps the flight bag. 'Come see.'

Nzinga's eyes widen as he produces a shimmering trove of blister packs: Maybelline Dream Bouncy Blush, a signed Maybelline Eyelash Curler, Maybelline Color Show nail polish, Maybelline Ultra Cake Blue Shadow eyeliner, Maybelline Rich 'n Gentle mascara, Maybelline Kissing Sticks.

Baptiste knows what to bring girls. He has a daughter, Nanchelle, who lives with her mother in an American city called Baton Rouge. Nzinga's never been to a city, but once, as a small child, she saw a town. It had been hastily evacuated, though there was no telling whether it was forced or voluntary. *Land can be held only after it has been captured a number of times*, a grim Maoism that Nzinga knew even then. She looked down the graded road that ran the length of the town, marveling at the permanence of the breeze-block walls, the window screens and glass, the dead street lamps. Her father forbade her to accompany his soldiers into the buildings while they cleared explosives hidden in mattresses, jewelry boxes, dolls. Toys are the enemy.

Nzinga stuffs the makeup into her rucksack. It's then that she realizes the Coke-can radio is missing.

B ase life means cooked meals, raised wooden tent floors, walled latrines, a donkey boiler for hot baths, the pleasant rote of school lessons, American Westerns projected onto the canvas wall of the clinic, generator-powered lights strung along paths that spider out from Papa's command tent, pushing back the forest darkness and keeping the leopards and hyenas at bay; an entire world miraculously created in the space of two days and pulled down in half the time. Base life is an ethereal place, bittersweet in its impermanence.

On the parade ground, Nzinga watches the dismantling. She's

standing front and right of the formation, the non-commissioned officer's position. Tee Baptiste calls attention, and thirty-six children snap to attention, their knees slightly bent to prevent circulation blackout. They're dressed in cut-off fatigue trousers and silk-screened T-shirts – *Pac-Man*, Ronald Reagan, *Star Wars*. Tee Baptiste paces along their ranks, the children arranged from shortest to tallest. He locks eyes with an eight-year-old, darts forward to make her flinch, tries not to smile when she doesn't.

There's a break in the clouds, the sky mirroring on the puddles. Tee Baptiste drags a wooden box the size of a child's coffin out onto the tailgate of the Bonanza.

'Who's had a special birthday since I was here last?' he asks.

Two boys and a girl raise their hands. He presents each with an M16 rifle, and they stuff their cargo pockets with empty banana clips and handfuls of bullets. *To rid the world of the gun, one must take up the gun.* Mamãe has been pressuring him to arm any child strong enough to shoulder a weapon.

Tee Baptiste marches the remaining children away like a drill sergeant, like a Pied Piper, into the perimeter forest, where they will stalk their mothers and sisters who stand guard, lion cubs on the prowl. The sentries pretend not to notice the brightly colored T-shirts inching toward them through the shifting grass.

That night, Nzinga reads *Teen* beneath a path light, while her parents quarrel inside the command tent.

Mamãe tells Papa he must order the cadre to counter-attack. '*If an army loses its initiative, it loses its liberty,*' she says, throwing Mao at him.

Papa argues for a mobile retreat and the resumption of base life. He quotes the Chairman back to her: *Victory is gained not through captured territory or enemy corpses, but rather in years and decades.* It's a running argument between the two, one that has lasted as long as Nzinga can remember. She flips through the magazine and wonders if American girls wear makeup all the time, or only on special occasions, like prom. She imagines herself riding in a limousine beside a boy in a tuxedo.

Her parents quarrel until the generator runs out of petrol and a brittle silence settles over the darkened camp. Nzinga closes her magazine and stares at the silhouette of the floating bridge that leads away from enemy lines, toward Zaire and the American Station in Kinshasa, the fount of Tee Baptiste's inexhaustible supplies.

A gainst all protocol, Nzinga returns for the Coca-Cola can radio. There's no harm in it, she's decided. The government soldiers are not disciplined enough to wait silently day and night, and there have been no reports from the villages of Cubans in the sector.

Still, she did not bathe that morning. The Cubans' sense of smell is keener than their eyesight, a well-known fact among base camp children. The commandos hunt in packs, like hyenas, barely maintaining sight with one another, morphing in the green of the forest, emerging only when it's too late. It's said they keep a rat from the sugar cane fields of their homeland as their unit mascot. They allow it to scurry the length of their mess table, its cunning eyes locked on the owner of the plate from which it has chosen to eat, its quivering whiskers dappling the surface of the sauce.

Nzinga pauses on the perimeter of the clearing, resumes her slow approach, scanning the ground for the red and white of the Coke can. A disquieting thought takes shape. *It's gone forever. No more Voice of America. No Tiffany, Wham!, Madonna.* She's so intent on finding the radio, she doesn't notice the glint of sunlight reflected in the lens of a sniper scope.

B urgos lies prone in a brake of leaves that has collected in the roots of the yellowwood, searching the night shadows for movement. At first he can think only of the heat, the loneliness of this assignment. He focuses on the moment, and then the next, until cadent time gives way to the arrhythmia of rainfall, the chorus of toads, leaves turning in the wind. This is the most important skill a commando can develop, the thing no one teaches in infantry training, the ability to wait silent and motionless. All the rest – parade craft, marksmanship, even courage – are nothing without patience. This is why he will survive this war to return to his wife and daughter, barring a blind bullet, an errant piece of shrapnel, some careless act of destiny.

Dawn filters through the canopy, illuminating spider webs and floating pollen, painting blue swathes across the forest floor. In shadow, Burgos's fatigue jacket is a muted gray, as is the rifle barrel that protrudes from the deadfall piled before him. His thoughts are as still as the mist. A centipede insinuates itself under the cuff of his fatigue jacket, its ciliary legs in communion with the fine hairs of his forearms. Monkeys converse overhead, branches bending with their weight, shaking tree-rain onto his ears and neck.

Some small movement registers on Burgos's optic nerve. His hand finds the rifle's pistol grip. And there it is again, an almost imperceptible rippling in the bush. He watches through the telescopic sight as a slight figure emerges into the clearing.

I t's nearly afternoon when Nzinga returns to base camp with her radio. She took a long route home, keeping clear of the track that leads to the camp, circling back to see if anyone was following. A heavy rain has washed away her footprints.

Only the command center remains, its octagonal canvas walls monolith amid the stumps of felled trees, the charred ground of dead bonfires, the flattened patches of earth where a village of tents once stood, the radiating footpaths, one of which Papa follows, confused and unquiet, stepping gingerly, as if through a cemetery.

Inside the command tent, Mamãe reads a thin volume of poetry, her lips moving as the lines sound in her head. Taped to the canvas wall above her is a photograph of a centuries-old woodcut: Nzinga the Warrior Queen drawing her great bow, the arrow pointed at some unseen enemy. Mamãe persists, over repeated protests, in cutting Nzinga's hair in the shape of a helmet, transforming her into a mirror image of her namesake.

'Can I help Tee Baptiste salt the track?' Nzinga asks.

Her mother is startled from her book. Poetry is her only indulgence

– not the crude décimas churned out by communists, peasants and Spaniards, rather the epic verses of Luís de Camões, João Villaret's spoken fados, the heteronyms of Fernando Pessoa. Her rationale for teaching poetry is not inconsistent with Mao's teachings on guerrilla warfare. *An army without culture is a dim-witted army, and a dim-witted army cannot defeat the enemy.*

'It's late. Can't he manage on his own?' Nzinga's mother doesn't like the American. She says he comes from slave stock.

Nzinga pleads with her eyes.

Mamãe's eyes drift back to her book. 'Go on,' she murmurs. 'We move out at sunset.'

B urgos watches through his riflescope as two old men secure tarps over a loaded lorry. He had followed the girl with the radio back to the base camp and called in the coordinates to his unit.

Some children push an old tire across the parade ground, unaware that they are playing in a crossfire zone. One of the girls is the same age as Burgos's daughter. *Politics is war without bloodshed, while war is politics with bloodshed.*

Forty-eight Cuban commandos lie motionless to the north and west of the dismantled base camp, their weapons trained on the women who guard the perimeter. The mortar crews quietly debate issues of pitch and distance, though they agree it will take at least three rounds before their shells reach the floating bridge. Burgos has positioned the Angolan troops on the far side of the stream where they can pick off any survivors who try to swim across, a simple enough mission.

He checks his wristwatch, hoping the terrorist commander will return with his soldiers. A village headman arrives in a pickup truck filled with fresh produce and dried game meat for the upcoming trek.

Earlier, the girl with the radio had climbed into the cab of an SUV driven by a well-fed man in a green beret. Burgos considered radioing their heading to brigade headquarters so that the Angolans might set an ambush, but he'd been briefed to avoid engaging Americans in combat whenever possible. And there was something innocent in the way the girl had held the radio to her ear that morning, swaying to a backbeat from across an ocean.

The old men climb into the cab of the lorry and a diesel cloud erupts from the tailpipe as the engine turns over. Burgos points a Very pistol at the rain clouds and looses a flare, its pop and sizzle closely followed by the hollow whoosh of mortar shells being launched from their tubes and the percussion of the opening fusillade. The sentries are dead before the flare completes its arc across the darkening sky.

During the succession of volleys, thousands of bullets crisscross the base camp on intersecting trajectories. Two tracer rounds collide midair, the odds of it so infinitesimal as to suggest some unseen purpose had not the projectiles careened aimlessly, one buried in the dirt, the other embedded in a tree trunk.

In the sweep of Burgos's riflescope, wholescale slaughter is revealed as a scroll of compressed images. Nothing has been accomplished beyond the death of a few dozen women, children and old men. The terrorist soldiers will exchange their fatigues for khaki trousers and graphic T-shirts and disappear into the villages. *The guerrilla moves among the people as a fish swims in the sea.* Some may be captured, others will return to civilian life. But most will rendezvous with their commander within the week. *We shall heal our wounds, collect our dead, and continue the fight.* Mao has shifted sides.

Burgos trains his rifle on a serval cat, frozen and panting, and fires low, throwing up dirt at its feet. The creature, startled from its paralysis, bounds into the forest.

There is a story Mamãe tells about her ancestors, a coastal people who harried slaving expeditions into the interior of Angola. The Portuguese called them Wreckers because it was said that they lit bonfires to lure ships onto the shoals, though any sea captain will laugh at the idea of steering toward a false light. Rather the bonfires served as a beacon for those too old or frail to be taken by the slavers, the village-less whose homes had been razed. The coastal people embraced the name, calling themselves Wreckers of Slavery, Wreckers of the Portuguese Empire, and though they suffered heavy casualties during their raids, their numbers were replenished by those they freed, until they became a tribe related not by the blood in their veins, but rather by the blood they spilled. Mamãe can recite the names of forty generations – forty-one counting Nzinga – going back to a distant ancestor, a fisherman who first sighted a slave ship anchoring offshore, two centuries of Wreckers, not one dead from old age.

Nzinga has no expectations that her life will end differently, though she's happy to be alive in this moment, the rain cool against her face as she walks to the parade ground where the Bonanza is parked, its driver asleep behind the wheel. The back of the SUV is now empty save for four wooden boxes, each containing four landmines. Tee Baptiste calls them Bouncing Betties, like something she might find in her Caboodles makeup case. She holds the Coke-can radio next to Tee Baptiste's ear and switches it on full volume, making him jump in his seat as Cyndi Lauper blares from the punctured speaker. Nzinga has placed a Band-Aid over the bullet hole, convinced that it was a stray round from the firefight.

She climbs into the passenger seat, studying Tee Baptiste as he drives out of the camp, his seat back, arm stretched languidly to the wheel, steering with one wrist. He reminds her of her uncle, who, like so many others in Papa's cadre, was killed by Cubans in the Battle of Cuito Cuanavale.

'You look more like us than the Afro-Americans in *Teen*,' she tells him.

'Lots of people in Louisiana look like Angolans,' he says. 'We come from here, way back.'

Every road and path is suspect, hundreds of thousands of landmines buried and forgotten after decades of colonial and civil wars. The government soldiers have taken to walking along the shoulders, the backs of their thighs aching with muscle tension, their testicles spooned by steel toes removed from the uppers of their combat boots.

Tee Baptiste pulls over, and Nzinga chooses a spot in the stunted growth that lines the track, unfolds her entrenching tool, and buries it into the dense earth. As she works, the American tells her that this is his last visit. He's out-processing from the army to retire on half-pay so he can live in Louisiana with his wife and daughter, Nanchelle.

Nzinga looks up from her digging, searches his eyes to see if he's kidding. She stretches a cloth measuring tape the depth of the hole. Thirteen centimeters.

Tee Baptiste shows her a photo she's already seen, his Vietnamese wife and the little girl who looks like him. 'I'm tired of dressing like a lizard,' he says, 'following regs, living wherever the hell the army decides to send me. Life is like shoes, Home Fry. If it's too small, it's going to pinch and squeeze.'

Nzinga removes a landmine from its box. It's stupid, she knows, but she always thought some day Tee Baptiste would take her to live with him and his family in Louisiana. She would be Nanchelle's big sister, and they could make up each other's faces, listening to a radio station whose deejay isn't always talking about freedom and resistance.

The Bouncing Betty looks like a large tin of beans. Nzinga removes the U-shaped safety clip, exposing the pressure plate embossed with an arrow and the letters *S*, for *safety*, and *A*, for *armed*. She rotates the pressure plate until the arrow is aligned with the *A*. Nzinga doesn't remember being taught how to plant a bounding mine any more than she remembers learning Mao quotes. The knowledge has always been with her, like the scene of her own premature birth, as told by her papa, each detail so vivid as to create a memory where none exists. It unfolds in the bed of a speeding lorry during the War of Independence from the Portuguese. An August wind streams beneath the canvas, softening the vibrato of Mamãe's moans as the spent shock absorbers jangle over the ungraded road. Mamãe leans on all fours against the wheel well, gooseflesh rising on her naked thighs, Papa's arm wrapped around her belly, and they breathe as one, awaiting the birth of their daughter. In actuality, Papa was far away conducting an attack on a railway station, Mamãe has made that clear. Yet the false memory persists, a conspiracy between father and daughter.

Nzinga pushes dirt into the hole until the pressure plate is covered.

'Thought you said you knew how to plant a landmine,' Tee Baptiste says. 'Ground all churned, prong sticking up like it's waving at you to keep away. Have to be blind to step on that.'

Nzinga's laughing again, enjoying being teased. She unearths tufts of grass and replants them around the landmine, the pressure prong now lost among the broad blades, and she smooths moss and wet leaves against the disturbed earth and over any footprints she's made.

'Check it out,' she says.

Tee Baptiste inspects her work from various angles. 'Damn girl. That's some nasty shit right there.'

Nzinga's proud, but uneasy. She's seen the amputees in the villages.

'Hey, Tee,' she says. 'What are you going to do when you go home to Louisiana, drive around in your Bonanza handing out rifles and Bouncing Betties to the locals?' Joking about his leaving makes it seem less true.

'Girl, you be bugging,' he says, then grows serious. 'I been saving up to open an Athlete's Foot.'

Nzinga gives him a blank stare.

'It's a store that sells all kinds of sports apparel, mostly shoes. I'm buying a franchise in the Acadiana Mall in Lafayette.' Tee Baptiste tries to describe *mall* to her as she plants the rest of the mines, but she lacks context to process the information.

Nzinga and Tee Baptiste are walking back to the Bonanza when they hear the distant explosions of mortar shells. He wraps an enormous hand around her bicep, preventing her from running toward the camp. She kicks out at him, bruising his ankles through the Givenchy boots, scarring the leather. Both remain silent, their struggle punctuated by concentrated gunfire, time measured in the intervals between volleys as the enemy reloads, its passage falling away altogether as unseen attackers target anything that still moves, the frequency of the reports tapering off as the enemy advances, dispatching anything yet alive until there is only the echo of a final round.

Nzinga hangs weightlessly in Tee Baptiste's unbreakable grip, suspended above the unfamiliar track that stretches away from, no longer toward, base camp, its direction suddenly reversed. Everything's gone: tents, floorboards, generators, cots, the donkey boiler, Mamãe's poetry books. This is all the loss she can process at the moment. A week later, sandwiched between two GIs on a military charter jet bound for Charleston, South Carolina, Nzinga will wrap her mind around all the rest of it.

Burgos argues with a brigade commander as they approach the village near the decimated base camp. The latter has just been informed of the headman who delivered food to the terrorists, and now he wants to raze the village.

'Arrest the headman and his sons,' Burgos tells the stubborn Angolan, 'but leave the village intact.' He tries to explain that a brutal response will only increase local support for the enemy. The brigade commander strides ahead, no longer listening.

But for this heated exchange, Burgos would have noticed the anomalies in the terrain, the darker patch of earth, the artfully planted grass concealing the exposed prong of a bounding landmine.

The weight of the brigade commander's foot activates the pressure fuse, the tick of the striker against the percussion cap unheard as it ignites a short delay, allowing time for the commander to step off. Burgos does hear the small charge that propels the landmine into the air, chest-high, as well as the larger explosion that follows. The sub-audible, high-velocity steel fragments do not register, nor does the blind shrapnel that slices through the breast pocket of his fatigue jacket, severing his atrial septum.

Enough oxygen remains in Burgos's still blood to sustain conscious thought for perhaps a minute. The earth is damp against his head. Raindrops roll across his open eyes, softening the outlines of inert and writhing Angolan soldiers. From this perspective, the casualty zone seems endless.

Fragments of memories spark and dim: his wife squinting up at him from the dock, her hair auburn in the sun, as he boards an Angola-bound troop transport; his grandfather offering him a crisp of golden skin sliced from a pig wedged between two screen doors over a roasting fire; the naked breast of an almost-forgotten girl; his father's open coffin; his newborn daughter, light in his arms; an Angolan girl with a Coke-can radio dancing in a forest clearing.

The oxygen is depleted, time lurches to a halt, and the girl in the forest becomes as still as a photograph.

Yellowwood trees stream past the passenger window of a Chevy Bonanza, their shapes dark and undefined. The odometer scrolls American miles, marking the ever-widening distance between Nzinga and base life.

'Take a good look,' Tee Baptiste says.

'There's nothing about this place I want to remember.'

'Can't unforget it,' Tee Baptiste tells her, 'no matter how you try. Everything you see is always in your mind.'

The dashboard radio is tuned to Voice of America. Nzinga, last of the Wreckers, listens to Prince with closed eyes, imagining herself in a red Corvette. They're en route to the American station in Kinshasa, where Tee Baptiste will put her on a C-130 bound for Ramstein Air Base, West Germany, there to be processed as a refugee and relocated to a foster family in Lafayette, Louisiana. In turn, her father will launch offensive operations against the communists.

The old man had come to witness her departure, sniffing around for some phony moment of intimacy. Mamãe was right after all. *Passivity is fatal,* Mao's incontrovertible truth.

The big Chevy engine rumbles on the other side of the firewall. *Mao's a drag,* Nzinga thinks, shocking herself. *Fuck Mao.* She opens the Caboodles case, gazes at the photo of the green-eyed girl taped inside the lid, the image blurred in the SUV's electric vibration. The Coke-can radio jitters across the floor of the cab, the bullet hole forgotten behind the Band-Aid. Nzinga turns the rearview mirror on herself, applies some blush. Soon she will live in a city in America, where she will call herself Maybelline, and she will be beautiful, like the makeup. ∎

Force Visibility

Everywhere we went, I went
in pigtails
no one could see—

ribbon curled
by a scissor's sharp edge,
the bumping our cars

undertook when hitting
those strips
along the interstate

meant to shake us
awake. Everywhere we went
horses bucking

their riders off,
holstered pistols
or two Frenchies

dancing in black and white
in a torn apart
living room

on the big screen
our polite cow faces
lit softly

by New Wave Cinema
I will never
get into. The soft whirr

of CONTINUOUS STRIP IMAGERY.
What is fascism?
A student asked me

and can you believe
I couldn't remember
the definition?

The sonnet,
I said.
I could've said this:

our sanctioned twoness.
My COVERT pigtails.
Driving to the cinema

you were yelling
This is not
yelling you corrected

in the car, a tiny
amphitheater. *I will*
resolve this I thought

and through that
RESOLUTION, I will be
a stronger compatriot.

This is fascism.
Dinner party
by dinner party,

waltz by waltz,
weddings ringed
by admirers, by old

couples who will rise
to touch each other
publicly.

In INTERTHEATER TRAFFIC
you were yelling
and beside us, briefly

a sheriff's retrofitted bus.
Full or empty
was impossible to see.

KOBANE: THE AFTERMATH

Lorenzo Meloni

Introduction by Claire Messud

If black is the colour of the Islamic State, then grey is the colour of destruction. In Lorenzo Meloni's extraordinary images, the mountains of rubble, the skeletal ruins, the dust-veiled avenues, even the scrubby plants in what was the city of Kobane emerge in overlapping shades of grey.

The life force, on the other hand – humanity – stands out against this landscape of despair, in murals, T-shirts and scarves of fuchsia, turquoise, crimson, sunshine yellow. The pre-war photographs Meloni has collected, marred by their own spidery explosions, depict a thoughtless technicolour world of flower-filled weddings and vibrant sunlit gardens; today, colour in Kobane is willed, almost defiant: children's bright sweaters glow in the concrete scree, a pair of balloons waver above a hospital bed.

In mid-September 2014, 130,000 people, most of them Kurds from the canton of Kobane in northern Syria, fled across the border into Turkey to escape advancing Islamic State forces. A four-month siege of the city ensued, during which the battle for Kobane was fought at close range by the Kurdish men and women of the People's Protection Units (YPG) and Women's Protection Units (YPJ), with the assistance of repeated coalition air strikes. Some civilian families remained in the city, huddled in basements, helping the effort as they could, unwilling to countenance defeat. In January 2015, the Kurds began to regain ground; on the 26th of that month, the Islamic State was routed and the city fully reclaimed by the YPG and YPJ.

What then? Some – even many – families have returned to their city, desperate to leave the refugee camps to which they'd been consigned; but they returned to unimaginable devastation. The cost of saving Kobane from the Islamic State has been enormous, not just in lives lost, but in the way of life itself, which has been altered beyond recognition. Where once there was a house, there is indecipherable debris; where there was a school, pocked walls and sliding piles of sodden paper; where there was a garden, scarred earth and denuded trees snapped like twigs.

In late June – exactly six months after their defeat – the Islamic State again attacked the city, massacring 146. They were again overrun, and Kobane's citizens have set about reclaiming and, one hopes, in time, rebuilding their homes.

Meloni, through his photographs, conveys not only the barren, jumbled vistas of this post-apocalyptic cityscape, but, movingly, the stirrings of quotidian normality that flicker in the chaos. We see a clutch of cheerful little girls, apparently at play. Two women attend them, one grasping a fir sapling that sprouts, incongruous, from the rubble, while the other appears lost in thought. We catch a mother as she feeds her twin babies on a makeshift mattress: she is dressed as if for a garden party, her hair caught up in a bun, her patterned frock elegantly draped over her crouching form. She turns to the window, to the light, in what may be alarm, her left arm holding behind her a bottle for the swaddled infant she can't, for now, see. The tiled floor is patterned, the wall behind her cratered and cracked. Scattered just beyond her reach lies a cell phone and cigarettes. In another photo, an older man sits, agog, in one of the Middle East's ubiquitous white plastic garden chairs, its seat carefully softened by a rug. He leans forward, as if in conversation or watching a game of chess. It's a familiar sight – he should be at a table, perhaps at a cafe or in a town square, surrounded by other men, smoking, talking, drinking coffee. But in Kobane last August, the rest of the scene had simply evaporated: this man waits alone, at the ready in his smart blue shirt, small and human between a giant tumbleweed of wires and a distorted metal carcass, the hollowed hulk of an apartment building looming deathly behind him.

Meloni's most straightforwardly beautiful photograph is also the most painful to behold: it depicts a man bathing in the Euphrates. He squats naked, almost gleaming, at the water's edge, head down, examining a shoreline demarcated by algae. The river's placid pale-blue wash reaches to one side; sand hills undulate in the background; keen vegetation bursts along the banks. There is no destruction visible here, no death; there is no broken concrete; nothing is grey. Meloni's image stretches before us in gentle, natural colour, beneath the vast, impeccable sky. How, we must wonder, can this exist beside the city's horrors? And how can the brave people of Kobane, who have lost so much, hope to retrieve not only a semblance of their modern lives but this, too – this ineffable, innocent pleasure in an undamaged land? What is the way forward from here? ∎

January 2015. A group of fighters exits Kobane to fight in the surrounding villages.

January 2015. After the liberation of Kobane, YPG and YPJ soldiers check the dead bodies of Islamic State fighters for explosive belts.

August 2015. Painting inside a destroyed building.

January 2015. Shop destroyed during the war.

August 2015. A woman walks on the rubble of her collapsed house.

August 2015. A family stands on what is left of their home.

August 2015. The remains of the veils used by civilians to protect themselves from Islamic State snipers.

August 2015. A view of Azadi Square, also known as Freedom Square, the main square in the city.

August 2015. Arin with her twin sons. She returned to Kobane four months ago.

August 2015. Sarrin area. A YPG fighter bathes in the Euphrates river, the last known YPG-held position.

August 2015. A man is seen from the rubble.

August 2015. A young boy working as a blacksmith.

August 2015. View of the eastern side of Kobane. Most of the fighting happened here, in attempts to control the border with Turkey.

August 2015. Sarrin area. House used as a base for YPG-supporting soldiers, originally from Denmark, Germany, the United Kingdom and the United States.

February 2015. 21-year-old YPJ fighter Hevshin Kobani with her unit, on the western front.

August 2015. A man sits among the rubble on the eastern side of the city, the area most affected by air strikes and fighting between the YPG and the Islamic State.

August 2015. A family in front of their house.

January 2015. Garden destroyed by the fighting.

August 2015. A boy plays amid the rubble on the eastern side of the city.

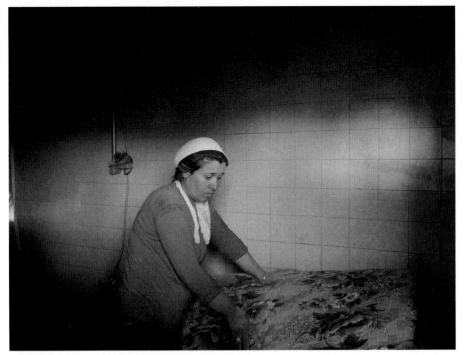

August 2015. A woman tries to recover some blankets from her house.

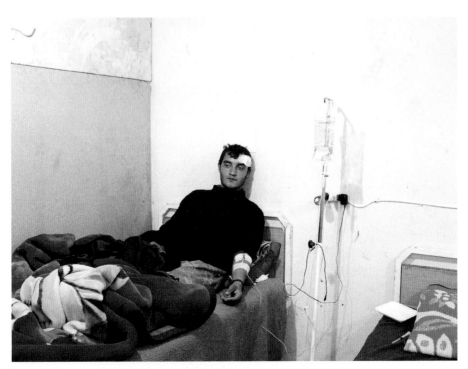

January 2015. A wounded YPG fighter in a field hospital.

August 2015. Destroyed school archive.

August 2015. A family waits inside the civilian hospital of al-Alam.

August 2015. A man attempts to salvage belongings from the ruins of his former home.

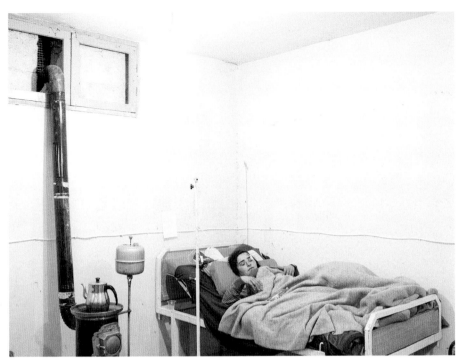

January 2015. A wounded YPJ fighter in a field hospital.

January 2015. The remains of Kobane's central market.

August 2015. The aftermath of an air strike on a building occupied by Islamic State forces.

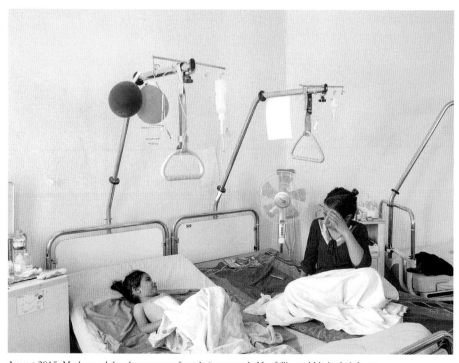

August 2015. Mother and daughter recover from being wounded by falling rubble in their home.

January 2015. Photographs found in the debris.

THE FERRYMAN

Azam Ahmed

My wife will tell me I smell of death tonight. She will leave two plastic tubs of water beside our door, one for my clothes and the other to bathe myself. She does not allow me to enter our home on nights like this, until I have shed the odor of the dead.

My friends snicker when they see the steaming tubs of water, which she heats to break the chill. They laugh because my wife tells me when I must clean myself. My neighbors respect me, though it is true that a woman directing a man is unusual. But these men do not know what I owe her.

Erasing the smell depends on the manner of death, and over the past five years I have become an expert. The odor of burn victims, for instance, is easier to erase when the burns are fresh. A simple bath will do. The scent of the decomposed requires many scrubbings before it goes. One must shampoo their beard and brush under their nails. You cannot overdo the rinsing.

In my village, I am an elder. Along with a few others, I make community decisions, handle disputes and am well regarded for my fairness. But behind my back, I know my people find me unusual. Children run up to me and bury their faces in my clothes, no doubt because their parents have told them of my occupation. Adults do not ask me the questions typical of our culture. My answers frighten them.

We are Pashtun farmers, all of us, growing pomegranates and grapes on fertile soil fed by the Arghandab River. Kandahar pomegranates are famous throughout Afghanistan, and we even send them across borders when the season is right. But I seldom farm anymore, not since the war picked up. Now my five sons tend our land, though they still ask me for advice sometimes to let me know I am not too old to help.

But this morning, as I finish my prayers, I receive a call from Commander Farhad. My wife is stirring in the kitchen, my sons preparing to leave the house for the day. The light of a yellow morning strikes the bread and sweet green tea my wife has laid out for me to eat.

'Malik, there has been a very serious air strike in Khakrez district,' he says right away. 'The Americans accidentally killed some of their own men, some of my Afghan police and maybe one or two Taliban.'

'Do you know how many and where exactly?' I ask, grabbing the disk of naan and tearing off a piece between my thumb and finger. Unlike my neighbors, I do not hate these foreigners. But I have seen their air strikes before, the fiery ruin, and lost friends to them. I cannot help but think there is justice in the Americans killing their own.

'Yes, there should be three of them. Their commander is here now, and he wants to know if you will help us,' he says, his breath growing heavier. 'As for where it took place, what does that matter? The whole district belongs to Raheem Gul.'

Then, softer, he says: 'Aziz Kako, it is important. The Americans are asking.'

What Farhad really wants is for me to help him win favor with the Americans. For officials, they are very useful people to have on your side. Powerful men in my province have solicited the Americans to settle disputes with their enemies. Others have become wealthy beyond imagination. Farhad thinks I will be as eager as him to help these foreigners. I am not.

'Fine,' I respond, letting go of my doubt. I set the piece of bread back down. 'I will try, but tell the American not to expect anything.'

When we have finished, I call Raheem Gul. Because there are Americans involved, the negotiation will be harder. He and I have a relationship, but these fighters are strange and unpredictable people. The years have hardened them beyond reason.

'Why should I turn over the bodies of these invaders to you?' Raheem Gul barks on the phone. I can usually tell when he is trying to provoke me and when he is being serious. Today I cannot.

He has never had his hands on the bodies of dead American soldiers, and I believe he is weighing their worth in his head. For a mid-level commander who spends nine months of the year in the dry mountains and deserts of the south, the ownership of American bodies is a powerful advantage.

'Because it is the same arrangement, with the Afghan government as with the Americans,' I explain, knowing it is untrue. For the most part, the deal is Afghans for Afghans, though sometimes there is a Pakistani or Uzbek. I once transported a white Chechen with hair the color of saffron and eyes of lapis. But the Americans will not be the same. And in truth, they are not to me, either.

Raheem Gul grows quiet and I know he is thinking it over. I eat during his silence, enjoying the dull salt and crunch of the bread and the sweet earthy flavor of the tea. He is not a stupid man. My personal request has both troubled and trapped him. I have done many things for him, driven to the rough edges of the province to collect the bodies of his fighters simply because he asked. He cannot easily tell me no.

'I will consider it,' he replies. 'There are Afghan forces too, which I will prepare for you to pick up. Then we can talk about the Americans.'

I have seen dead Americans before. A few years ago, I watched a bomb explode beneath one of their convoys as it passed through Kandahar, breaking open the side of one of their giant, sand-colored trucks. Heavy smoke filled the area. People gathered nearby, afraid to help. Eventually, the survivors pulled two bodies from the wreckage, one burned black, the other twisted like a child's toy.

The drive to Khakrez district is a stretch of endless brown desert, with hardly a color or feature to entertain the eyes. The nomadic Kuchi tribes occupy much of the land because it is no good for farming.

Two years ago, the Americans built a road through Khakrez, the kind of project that changed the way Afghans looked at them. And not in a good way. The district governor made a fortune, along with the Taliban commander he paid to allow the construction to go forward. But today, at least, I am grateful for it. The paved road makes the trip easier for Bilal, my long-time driver, and me.

In the car, Bilal listens to Pakistani music. The heavy thumps rattle his broken speakers as we drive over the naked land between Arghandab and Khakrez. I warn him that we must turn the music off once we get further into the district: the Taliban will not like it. He nods, then lights a cigarette, another vice the Taliban forbid.

My youngest son sometimes asks what life under the Taliban was like. I tell him this story: when they arrived in our village, they captured the mad dog Ruhullah, a warlord who severed the hands of farmers who refused to give him crop payments. The fighters made him walk on his hands and knees with a rope around his neck like a leash. When everyone had gathered, a gunman put a Kalashnikov to his head and pulled the trigger, without a word. They left his body in the square for three weeks.

Bilal and I arrive early at our destination, which I do not like. We pull off the side of the road into an open field of brush and stone north of the district center. The Taliban are a suspicious lot and they will ask more questions if we are here waiting for them. Air strikes have made them paranoid. Bilal opens his door to release the heat. He stares out at the run of the land searching for signs of smoke to tell us where the air strike hit and therefore the direction we will be heading. Distance is hard to gauge here.

An old Toyota hatchback pulls up with five men inside, their machine guns tucked between them. Raheem Gul steps out of the front passenger seat and motions for me to come over to his vehicle.

'How long have you been here,' he asks me, scanning the sky.

'Five minutes,' I say. 'The road was faster than we expected.'

Raheem Gul says nothing, continues looking at the cloudless blue overhead. He motions two of his men over. They squeeze out of the car, adjusting their gun straps with the empty eyes and stone faces that I have come to know these men by.

The men search us. They slide their hands into my pockets, pulling out my identification papers, money and telephone. They scan my phone for recent calls and run their hands over my waist and legs to make sure I have no tracking devices on me. When they are satisfied, they look to Raheem Gul.

'Get in the back seat,' he tells them. 'You, too,' he says, pointing at me.

In the vehicle, Raheem Gul says nothing. Bilal has thankfully cut the radio and hidden his cigarettes. We follow his men's vehicle, cutting through the bumpy plains toward the horizon. I will not ask about the Americans again, at least not now. My question will only make him more defiant.

Villages appear to the north, built of the same earth that sits beneath them. There is little evidence of life: no animals, no crops, no people. Everything hidden behind thick mud walls. After twenty minutes, we see a thin stick of smoke rising beyond the road, evidence of a large bomb.

Over a ridge, I can make out the contours of a crater, maybe a kilometer from a village I do not know. The driver in front is very careful now. He has slowed his vehicle and moved off the road, tracing the map of roadside bombs planted to keep out the unwelcome.

We drive like this for ten minutes before we enter the village, where a small gathering sits outside the mosque. The men are wrapped in white cloth to shield them from the open sun. Raheem Gul walks Bilal and me to the entrance where Farhad's police have been placed in the courtyard. Their bodies are torn apart. In some cases, body parts are piled on top of torsos. It smells of iron and explosives.

'You can start with these,' Raheem Gul says, kicking off his sandals to enter into the mosque. 'My men can help you.'

Bilal and I begin with the more complete remains. There are two. The villagers have laid the corpses on wool blankets and we grab the edges and start the difficult work of bringing them to the vehicle. Thankfully the attack is recent, and the rot has not set in yet. The heat from the blast must have sealed the wounds, because there is little blood. Raheem Gul's men watch us without saying anything.

Not to be offered tea is considered an insult in our culture, but I do not take offense in circumstances like this. Bilal winks at me moments later when Raheem Gul emerges from the mosque with a thermos and tray of glasses. We finish loading the second full corpse into the trunk, a young man with a faint dusting of facial hair, and Raheem Gul pours the tea.

'They will finish with the last two or three,' he says, pointing at the pile of body parts. His men say nothing but begin grabbing the arms and legs and stacking them in the center of the blanket. They take the corners of the cloth and tie them together in knots over the center of the remains, forming a bundle. Then two of them heave the package up and walk to my car while Raheem Gul makes his way out of the courtyard and onto the street.

Outside, the sun is bearing down in full strength. Another day and the smell of the bodies would fill the entire village. Raheem Gul looks in the direction of the crater, where the traces of smoke have started to fade. He has left the Americans down there. We will negotiate on site.

The walk down to the crater is not far, but requires making our way through the village. The mud walls hug the edges of the footpath, each compound bordering the next. Farmers have irrigated water through a channel that flows downhill. A dull mountain leans overhead.

There are few villagers outside at this hour. The men will be in the field, the women and children inside their homes. These are all Pashtun families living under the thumb of the Taliban. For them, there is no government and what little they see of it is corrupt and immoral, two things no Afghan can openly accept.

Past the village we come to another road, also unpaved. Raheem Gul walks in the exact center of it and I fit my shoes into his footprints until we have reached a slight valley where fields stretch into the distance.

'There,' he says, drawing his long arm in front of him, pointing to a small mound to the side of the crater. 'You can see your friends.'

Raheem Gul wants to insult me, but I do not mind. Many of his men died and he is angry at my dispassion, my willingness to aid those who brought fire from the sky. For the Pashtun, this is treachery. We fight one another as men. To have our lives taken from above, without warning or even a chance to survive, is an act of God. That the fire comes from the infidels burns him inside as well.

'Will we be able to bring the car down here?' I ask, pushing him to accept my request to collect the bodies. 'Carrying them up the hill will be very difficult for Bilal and me.'

'Who said you can take them?' Raheem Gul asks, scanning the field where a father and son are harvesting wheat. 'I do not think we will even bury them.'

Even Raheem Gul, a hard and bitter man whose compassion has been scrubbed away, sees that this is the ultimate disrespect. Even he cannot hate the Americans so much.

'Even for them, you must perform the burial,' I say. 'Even if you do not let me take them.'

'*Whoever then acts aggressively against you, inflict injury on him according to the injury he has inflicted on you,*' Raheem Gul recites, countering my words with those of the Quran.

Raheem Gul sees only those with blood on their hands as righteous. I am a useful tool, a necessary figure in the long war, but he does not respect me as a Muslim. I am not a fighter. He will try to batter me with verses, but I will show him how I fight.

'*The repayment of a bad action is one equivalent to it. But if someone pardons and puts things right, his reward is with Allah,*' I say back to him, challenging the depth of his faith.

Before he can respond, I have another ready: '*And good and evil*

*are not alike. Repel evil with that which is best. And lo, he between whom
and thyself was enmity will become as though he were a warm friend.'*

Raheem Gul turns to me. He grabs the length of his beard with
a gnarled hand and clears his throat. I have pushed him very far,
perhaps too far.

'Will we trade verses then, Malik?' he asks with a slanted smile.
'Come, let us see them.'

We walk the remaining distance, roughly two fields, to the site
of the blast. The dead Americans are stacked on top of one another,
stripped of their weapons and armor. There are three of them and
they look smaller than the ones I saw in Kandahar. They are like
children now, alone.

'They don't even know what they are fighting for,' Raheem Gul
tells me. 'Why should they be honored?'

'Burial is not an honor,' I say, feeling almost sad for him. 'It is
your duty as a Muslim.'

A man is cutting wheat with his son in the distance. There is no
wind to cool them, but they will carry on until the call to prayer.

'I know you would like to take these men back with you, Malik,
but I cannot help you,' Raheem Gul says before making his way up
the hill. 'Their bodies will remain here so they can count their losses
as we count ours. You will take those Afghan puppet soldiers with
you, but the Americans will stay.'

I do not follow Raheem Gul back to the mosque, and he does not
call me up. I squat beside the bodies instead. Their smell is starting to
emerge. In a day or two, the odor will be so strong the farmers will halt
their harvest. In five years, I have buried 748 men and I can tell you
this: we are all hardened by this misery. Some have lost sons. Others
land. But there is nothing so rigid as a man robbed of his humanity.

No one will remove the corpses until Raheem Gul gives his
permission, a cruelty forced upon everyone. He is finished with our
negotiations. He will expect me to leave soon but will not insult me by
escorting us out. He has given enough insult for one day.

At the top of the hill, I see him enter the mosque with his men, who leave their weapons at the door, leaning against the outer wall. Such men divide their time between fighting and praying, two things that could not be more different. I wonder what that does to them, if it explains them somehow.

I make my way back up the hill, tracing the footsteps of Raheem Gul once more. I say salaam to a few of the villagers along the way. A man missing his right arm below the elbow carts a bucket, a strip of fabric tied to its edges and slung over his body. The azan begins suddenly. Although I know it is time for noon prayers I have forgotten Bilal is waiting for me outside of the mosque. He will not join the Taliban for Zuhr prayer. He blows over a cup of steaming chai and takes a short sip.

'They have all gone for prayer,' Bilal says.

I scan the area for any of Raheem Gul's men. If the mullah spends a long time on the Khutba, it could be half an hour before they return. Prayers last longer on Friday. Bilal takes another sip as he watches me.

'What did Raheem Gul say,' Bilal asks.

'He will not give us the Americans,' I say. 'He will not even bury them.'

'Farhad will not be happy,' Bilal says, laughing. 'He will have to find another way to feed on American dollars.'

'I don't give a damn about Farhad,' I fire back at Bilal, who jumps at my words.

'Come, we have work to do.'

I have no special love for the Americans, or desire to make Farhad appear more useful to his military friends, but I will claim these bodies. The Quran tells us to look neither east nor west but to believe in Allah and spend of ourselves on the needy, whether orphans, wayfarers or captives of war.

'Malik, do not be too clever,' Bilal warns me. 'Where are you going?'

He pours his tea onto the ground and pops up beside me. I start walking down the path again, scanning for footprints in the dry earth.

'Wait,' I say, retracing my steps back to the wall of the mosque. 'The guns.'

Bilal backs away and shakes his head.

'Are you crazy, Malik?' he asks. 'He will kill us before we leave.'

'Then he will be forced to do so without his guns,' I say. 'Get the car.'

Bilal stands in shock, his head tilted slightly, holding his empty cup. In our three years together, he has never questioned my judgment, never hesitated. We once spent three days carting the corpses of fifteen dead Taliban, swollen with rot and fluid, into the pink deserts of Registan. We have traveled the whole of the south in his yellow taxi, carrying the bodies of the war dead for all sides: soldiers, police, Taliban and now, I think, the Americans. What Raheem Gul does not understand is that you cannot draw a line. I do not do this work for the government, or the Taliban, or even the men who I collect from the battlefield and return to their loved ones. All these years I have done this for God.

Raheem Gul and I are not dissimilar in that way, only he does not see it. While he prays we will see who does God's work. I collect the weapons, five in all, and put them in the back seat between the bodies of the Afghan police.

Bilal opens the driver's side door of the car and sits himself down, leaning his head over the steering wheel. He knows I will not back off. He turns on the car and slowly begins to follow me down the path.

This is our routine – I walk the route I have been shown, and he trails closely behind. You would think that tire tracks would not be able to trace the steps of a man, but once I have the course I am an expert at seeing the signs of disturbed earth that signal buried bombs.

We make our way down the hill, past a few farmers still on their way to the mosque for salat. They look at us with semi-interest; a funny old man walking down their hill while a yellow taxi follows him like a lost sheep. A few offer quiet salaams to us. My heart knocks in my chest the farther we go. Over the loudspeaker, the afternoon prayers begin.

Raheem Gul is a powerful man with friends across Kandahar, and the Taliban have long memories. I will go to Quetta if we make it out and plead my case there. Perhaps my old friend Muheeb will even forgive me. My wife will ask me about my day when I come home tonight, and I will tell her what I have done. She will think me stupid. She will tell me I have killed her husband and that she is now a widow. She will not be wrong to tell me these things.

At the site, Bilal opens the back of his taxi and spreads another blanket over the remains of the Afghan officers. We are close enough to the bodies that anyone who was wondering what we were doing now knows our plan. I do not look back up the hill. It will only distract us.

Bilal fits a blue pair of rubber gloves over his hands. The bodies have been stacked along the edge of the blast crater. The top one is in good shape, having avoided the worst of it. His skin is white like bread, dusted in a coating of black powder. I am surprised to see a boy not much older than my son in this uniform that once frightened all of us.

Bilal and I grab him from either side, beneath the chest with one hand and his left and right leg with the other, like a sack of grain. We toss the body onto the blanket. The Khutba is starting now, giving us perhaps fifteen minutes before the men notice their guns are gone. The topic is suffering and death, oddly appropriate. Though it is foolish, I stop to listen.

'Every soul will taste death,' the mullah says, reading from the Holy Quran. The men in the mosque, Raheem Gul and his followers, know more than the taste of death, I think. They have feasted on it and it has soured their ability to appreciate anything else.

It has soured mine, too, but in a different way. I can no longer eat cooked meat. The smell makes me ill. My wife cooks our rice and vegetables without lamb or chicken, a meal most Afghans would find poor. I think of her now, hanging wet clothes in the courtyard, boiling the pilau for dinner, heating the water for my bath over an open fire with bricks on either side to hold the pot.

Bilal grabs me by the arm and shakes me.

'Malik, what the hell are you doing?' he whispers, jerking his head in the direction of the car.

I scan the horizon, searching for villagers racing down the hill.

It is too early for that, I think. Bilal hurries over to grip the next body. This one is slightly larger, and his skin is black, not from burns or coal, but from God.

The final body is far heavier, and more destroyed than the others. This man must have been close to the blast because his arms dangle loosely, the flesh of his insides exposed. Bilal grabs another wool blanket from the car and we roll the American onto it. His face stares at me as we lift him with the sheet. For some reason his body has decomposed faster than his friends'.

Bilal lights a cigarette as we place the final body in the car and shut the trunk.

'We must hurry,' I tell Bilal. I can see movement atop the hill. A small gathering of elders and young boys are leaving the mosque.

Bilal starts the car and we take the dirt road around the village, which connects to the field about a half-kilometer from the blast site. We cannot afford to drive through the village again – even without their weapons the Taliban can stop us easily. But we do not know this other path, which will have more bombs buried in it.

Bilal is trying to balance careful driving with our need to flee. Coming down the hill, a few of Raheem Gul's men race after us, some with shovels, others with hoes. I grab Bilal's arm. He manages a smile and turns on his music, then turns it up as high as he can. The Pakistani pop screams from the windows as he races down the road. I catch a glimpse of Raheem Gul just before we break around the bend of the hill. I believe I see him smile, though not in a happy way.

When we are back on the highway, Bilal lets out a frightened laugh and turns down the music. I would like to tell him that I will take full responsibility for what we have done, but the gesture would not matter. He will pay, as I will.

I ask Bilal to stop by a culvert in the road, walk around the back of our car and begin pulling the rifles from the trunk. I carry all five down the steep bank and toss them into the dry tunnel beneath the road. I will call Raheem Gul, perhaps tomorrow, and tell him where I have hidden his weapons.

Inside the car, Bilal sighs. He is disappointed that I have left the guns, but he knows why and will not question my actions. We may have stolen the American bodies, but we are not thieves. I dial Farhad's number.

'Do you have news, Malik?' he asks, answering on the first ring.

'We are driving to the city now and should be arriving within a half-hour,' I respond.

'You have all three of them?' he continues.

'Please make sure the gates of the police compound are open,' I say before hanging up. I have never spoken to the commander like that before, but I am in no mood to accommodate him.

I am sure the Americans are pressuring him, perhaps even threatening him, to get their bodies back. I am certain it is no Afghan filling him with fear.

'Will they kill us, Malik sahib?' Bilal asks, plucking another cigarette from his pack.

'I don't know,' I say. 'Our fate is in the hands of God.'

As Afghans, we say this on cue, as a matter of course, though its meaning differs every time. Will I make it to the wedding? If God wills it. Can you lend me your car? If God wills it. Will the harvest be fruitful this year? If God wills it.

'Farhad better have a suitcase of money for us,' Bilal says, blowing smoke from his window. 'What do you think, Malik? Will we be rich?'

'If God wills it, Bilal,' I say, smiling.

When we pull into the compound, Farhad is outside, agitated and pacing. The Americans are not with him, but their vehicles are parked in front of his office and several of their soldiers stand around it, smoking. They do not look at us.

Bilal parks away from them, but close to the entrance. He scans the American faces, then Farhad's, and grunts. I know what he is thinking: he is disappointed that these soldiers are the ones he risked his life for. They look nothing like the fragile bodies we stole an hour earlier.

Farhad runs up to the car and opens my door.

'You have done well, Malik,' he tells me with an embrace. As he hugs me, he peers into Bilal's trunk to count the bodies. 'Our friends will be very happy. I am sure they will reward you.'

The Americans offer no help as Bilal and I begin removing the bodies. A few gather nearby to watch; some curse silently, others shake their heads. I cannot fathom their grief – I have not seen it, and these are a people whose inner lives are strange to me. We lay the bodies on the ground, over another cloth that Bilal has unfolded.

Farhad rushes me to his office where the Americans are waiting. I pull back and reach once more into Bilal's car for my pato. I snap it open and cover the dead Americans with it, enough so that their faces are not exposed to the sun. One of the soldiers, a bit older than the rest, watches me. He nods slightly.

Inside Farhad's office, the Americans are sitting on his couches with their boots on, legs spread wide. They have steaming cups of tea and platters of raisins and nuts. A picture of President Karzai, flanked on either side by bouquets of plastic flowers, is mounted on the wall behind Farhad's desk.

The men do not rise when we enter the room.

'My friends, Mr Malik has collected the bodies of your men from Khakrez,' Farhad tells the Americans, who seem to barely register the news when translated. 'They are outside now, for you to take back to your base.'

The Americans stand. One rubs his hand on his pants before sticking it out for me to shake. The other stands off to the side, staring out of the window at the trucks. Their translator, a young boy dressed in the American military uniform, waits for the Americans to respond. They do not. He and Farhad look at one another with the panic shared by men who depend on these Westerners.

'How'd he find 'em,' one of the Americans asks the translator.

'I know the commander in the area,' I reply. Farhad nods in agreement, watching the faces of his American friends. 'I have brought his men's bodies back to him in the past.'

The American curls his lips and nods, as if I have told him that I am a Taliban myself.

'So let me get this straight – you deal with the Taliban directly, go into their areas, bring them their dead, and you're not a Taliban?' Farhad's face is frozen in a mock smile, his eyebrows raised.

The American is standing with his hands on his hips, his chin out. His colleagues say nothing, their faces as blank as water. I consider telling the story of how we came to collect the bodies, the price we have paid to return these corpses. But I do not.

'Don't you know?' I say to the American, to the translator, to Farhad. 'We are all Taliban.'

Farhad lets out a chirp. The translator, I can tell, will soften my words. I ask the boy not to.

For a moment, the room is silent. Then, in a sudden burst, like he is choking, the American starts laughing. He closes his eyes, bends slightly at the waist, almost as if he is crying. His friend remains silent, but his posture eases.

'Well, hell,' he says to the translator. 'That's the damn truth.'

Without another word, the Americans leave the room. Farhad, stunned by the sudden departure, stares at me for a moment and then follows behind them. Outside, the Americans collect the bodies, place them in the back of a large truck and speed off towards their base, about six kilometers down the road.

I pluck my pato from the ground, where it has been tossed, and bundle it in my arm. Farhad continues to stare at the trucks as they vanish into traffic. He has lost face because of the Americans; even he cannot deny this. I will not press him, or stay for tea or an explanation. I will go home to my wife and tell her what I have done, what has happened.

She will scold me and then serve me food and tomorrow I will await more calls. ∎

AFTERMATH

Peregrine Hodson

It's stopped. The buildings have gone, the streets are rubble – and now there's nothing.

Silence.

At last, the war's over.

Only it isn't. The destruction, the horror and the misery repeat themselves – the same images, the same soundtrack – explosions, scared faces, sirens and pools of blood. Talking heads comment on the latest butchery in solemn tones, and everyone's sick of it.

The bodies came home, then the soldiers came home. Everyone was relieved the war was over – people were looking forward to getting on with their lives – but things turned out differently. We seem to be in unknown territory. Security and media pundits proclaim another kind of war – a struggle that could go on for a lifetime, for generations – the beginning of an epoch of perpetual war.

So? Maybe it was ever so.

From the remote past, a bit of mental flotsam – a semi-fact that's somehow found a way to lodge itself in memory: 'In the last two thousand years there have only been thirty-three years of total peace in the world – with no war anywhere.'

This may be fiction – how could anybody know, for God's sake? – but it holds a truth. It's hard enough getting a person out of a war

– it's harder getting the war out of the person. Whether we wish it or not, memory is faithful as a shadow. We forget that when memory goes, we go. Without memory, we're nothing. Somehow, we have to find a way to balance life with memory.

T his is the time of year when the past comes back with a special clarity. The sun's lower in the sky, closer to the horizon. The light's yellow with dust from the harvest, and everything – the stream and the trees and the hills beyond – seems to shine with an almost biblical radiance – just like Afghanistan, at this time of year, in the mountains. The sunlight's at the same angle, the leaves are beginning to turn, and by now there's probably snow in the higher passes. Time's running out, food supplies are low, and there's still a long way to go – over the Hindu Kush – before there's even a chance of a hot bath and some creature comforts.

It was a terrible journey, yet the images from that time are like glimpses of another, earlier existence – in spite of everything, there is still a bright, savage innocence.

The past surfaces unpredictably. Sometimes memory is so immediate the past seems no distance at all. A sight, maybe, a sound or a scent, and in less time than it takes to think, one is in the vanished moment – present in the past.

With luck, memory can be as wonderful as Proust's delight – the unexpected rediscovery in the fragrance of a morsel of madeleine – a miraculous epiphany. But memory is unreliable. It has a will of its own, and we're not entirely in control of it.

A barbecue – the smell of burning in the summer air – and, for a second or two, a forgotten corpse is horrifyingly present in the middle of a conversation with a neighbour about the weather.

Swallow – swallow again – and nod.

Smile.

The moment passes.

Memory slyly conceals itself in the details of daily life – in the fragrance of overripe melons, or the buzz of flies – so, *multum in parvo*, small things may have great significance. A name or a word can be the entry to another dimension. Once in that other place – an invisible space exactly parallel to everyday existence – it can take some time to get back. It's like those stories where benighted travellers lie down to sleep on a grassy bank, then wake – years later – to discover everything's changed around them. Where has the time gone? What happened? Who am I now?

In that other, unseen dimension – a world between worlds – normal time's irrelevant. Time, if it exists, has a different meaning. Everything is subject to the law of necessity – apparently, there is no choice. Survival. One has to survive – there must be a way – somehow, one has to find the trail. So the search begins, once again, and the hunt is on – it continues until one finds whatever one's trying to find – nothing else matters. Deeper than hunger, this is the brute imperative of instinct – one has caught the scent and so one keeps on returning to it like a dog.

I love this time of year in Japan. I think of the autumn light in Kyoto, the colours of the maple trees – yellow as gold, and red as blood – and the wood-ash scent of incense in the courtyard of Buddhist temples. I remember the beginning of Matsuo Bashō's memoir poem, *The Narrow Road to the Deep North*: 'The sun and moon are the travellers of eternity. The years that come and go are also travellers.'

The years may forgive or forget, but our nature condemns us to remember – even things we wish to forget.

For some time now I've been experimenting – in an utterly unprofessional way – with the past. I've been trying to find a way to recreate what's been lost or forgotten. I carefully examine the fragments I discover – looking for a pattern, trying to make sense of what remains – and maybe find a meaning in what happened long ago.

Time can heal. This is the approximate limit of what I've learned so far. But it can also take time for a wound or a disorder to become apparent. With hindsight, maybe someone with the right skills and experience could have recognised what was happening earlier. But it was different then – there wasn't the level of knowledge there is now – and, unintentionally, I probably helped to delay the diagnosis.

I first realised something was different in Japan. I was working as an investment banker in Tokyo, a girlfriend had come out from England to join me, and we were at one of the summer festivals the Japanese love to celebrate with fireworks. The moon was a perfect parody of the round paper lanterns that still sometimes hang outside old-fashioned Japanese restaurants – pale pink in the last of the sunset, tinged by the chemical glow of the sky over Tokyo. In the twilight, the still-warm air was pungent with the smell of explosives. A chrysanthemum of light blossomed above our heads, a mandala of fire disintegrating in a thunder flash – and another, and another – and then, without warning, the red and white stars dissolved in a watery mist.

What was happening? I was having a great time – fantastic fireworks, in love with a beautiful girl – so why was I crying? These weren't tears of joy – they were spontaneous, yet strangely emotionless – more like the tears from peeling an onion, a physical reaction to external stimuli. Tara's upturned face was in profile, lit by another golden chrysanthemum opening above us. She sensed my gaze, and turned towards me. She asked why I was crying, and I said I didn't know.

As a boy, I used to hear about men who had a bad time during the war, who did funny things when they heard loud noises. At school there was a master with a short fuse – he'd been at the D-Day landings – and the classroom door slammed with a bang could trigger a volcanic eruption. In our free time we practised the perfect accidental grand slam that would transform the gently humorous man into a red-faced gargoyle of rage.

And the grand slam worked – every time.

My grandfather was also marked by war. He went to Gallipoli in 1915, where he was hit in the hip by a dumdum bullet. Unable to move, he lay in no man's land for two days and nights, until his sergeant crawled through the wire to find him, and dragged him back to safety.

Thirty years later, the after-images of war still troubled my grandfather. My mother told me about his first meeting with his prospective son-in-law, my father. The omens were ambiguous – there was mutual goodwill, but the older man and the younger man were natural opposites.

Before Gallipoli, my grandfather was in the Scottish rugby team. After the war, he worked in the family business – a company making mining machinery – until eventually, decades later, he was chosen to run the company.

Mining wasn't in my father's blood. Nor was business, or money. He was an artist who'd published a slim volume of poetry. He could draw wonderful cartoons of cats and dogs, he was witty and amusing, but he was a different kind of man from my grandfather, waiting in his study after a long day, whisky in hand. My father, young and fashionably dressed, stepped forward nervously to meet his future father-in-law. He was wearing bright red socks. My grandfather greeted my father warmly, then he noticed the scarlet socks. He paused – and without another word he left the room.

The moment my grandfather caught sight of my father's socks – that terrible flash of scarlet – is vivid in my mind's eye, as bright as anything I've seen in life.

A photograph of my grandfather shows a young man in uniform, barely into his twenties, with long eyelashes and a modest, neatly trimmed moustache. Months later, the bullet shattered his hip, narrowly missing the femoral artery.

What happened in no man's land? How did the experience shape the man, and influence his first impression of my father? As a classicist, my grandfather probably knew the Greek origin of the word 'character': meaning an impression made by something – a seal, or signet ring – in clay or wax. But how much of someone's character is formed by force of circumstance – and how much by design?

My grandfather kept the shirt of a friend killed beside him in

Gallipoli – the shirt had been cleaned, but the stains were unmistakable – and it remained among his clothes until the day he died. As a small boy, I was naturally thrilled to hear about this authentic relic of war – and secretly disappointed to learn my grandmother burned the shirt after my grandfather's death.

Blood and fire – the ancient elements of war – recur through the generations.

M y father could make people helpless with laughter. He saw the absurdity – the utterly pointless rigmarole of the daily dance – and he loved to share the absurdity with others. In this, he was more cartoonist than artist. He was a lanky youth in the Home Guard when the Germans were bombing Bath. On duty during a raid, he found a woman hanging by her legs, trapped in the wreckage of her house. Somehow, he supported her on his shoulders through the night, while the bombs fell and the city burned, until at dawn a rescue party found them. The woman died of her injuries soon afterwards, and my father received a commendation for his courage.

Was that night without sleep the reason why my father was always so sensitive to noise?

My own alertness to certain sounds may be inherited, learned or epigenetic. Whatever the reason, like my father I prefer the quiet of the country – even if the peace is sometimes broken by the noise of planes or helicopters.

M y tearful episode at the firework display in Tokyo was puzzling at the time, but it didn't really bother me – and thinking it over later, the cause was obvious. In the split second of light as the golden chrysanthemum opened, the sudden flash of brightness might have been a Russian flare in Afghanistan.

Travelling by night, we did our best to avoid Russian patrols – they knew we were somewhere in the darkness, but they couldn't see us. On moonless nights they were particularly alert – or nervous – and flares were more frequent. A fiery trail grazed the darkness, a stark, cold glare, whiter than moonlight, lit up the landscape. The light transfixed us, turning us into statues of stone-like shadow, waiting for it to end in a burst of gunfire, or darkness.

Maybe the noise contributed in some way – the physiological effect of the sound – but whatever it was, the tears were gone soon enough, and it hardly seemed serious. The involuntary response was simply an oddity – a minor side effect of previous excitement – and I didn't think any more about it.

A few months after the firework festival, I began to write a book about Afghanistan. The book was a modest success, and it seemed as if the Afghan chapter of my life was over.

But, sooner or later, the past comes back – and, one way or another, we remember.

The sun is shining, and the sea is the colour of lapis and emerald – tantalisingly brilliant, like the Mediterranean – only it's winter, on the Isle of Harris, off the north-west coast of Scotland.

Investment banking's another world away – my time as an analyst is over – and I'm free.

Apart from a scattering of rubbish tossed up by winter gales, almost everything here is shaped by nature. The coast is shattered by Atlantic storms, the rocky hills and outcrops eroded by wind and rain – it's a place scoured by the elements. Here, change is measured by the centuries of birth and death in the weather-worn tombs of the kings of Scotland, or by the millennia of the great stone circle of Callanish, with its secrets still waiting for the light. A gentle breeze is blowing, and the waves are rolling in towards the shore. I catch a whiff of something unexpected in the salty air, and without thinking – instantly – I'm there. The dusty rubble buzzing with flies, the invisible aura of the men wearing clothes taken from the bodies of dead Russians – the smell is so close to present reality I tell myself it has to be a hallucination.

A brief, involuntary wave of nausea – then it's okay, it's under control.

But why is that smell here – of all places?

The thought, like the sweetly satanic stench in my nostrils, won't go away. I consider the possibilities – a drowner, maybe – some poor wretch off a ship registered in Panama, or a fisherman torn overboard in a storm. A few paces further on, I reach the crest of a dune and see, half-buried in the sand, the innocent cause of the miasma – the rotting carcass of a seal, black and glistening in the sunlight.

We might hope to avoid the consequences of our actions, but chance is inevitable. Trapped like Jonah by coincidence, the past catches up with us – if one's unlucky, one may be engulfed.

If one's lucky, daylight may come again.

M y son was in bed upstairs and his mother was reading to him. I was watching a documentary about the Great War. The flickering black-and-white film showed a series of men in uniform, all clearly suffering from some kind of disorder. One stared blankly into the camera, another with a clear, steady gaze seemed perfectly normal – except for the spasm intermittently contorting the muscles of his face.

A clip of a man walking was bizarrely fascinating. Filmed in profile, the man was standing to attention – he stepped forward but, just as he was about to put his foot to the ground, he lifted it abruptly – then lowered it again gently. He stood – as if waiting for a signal – then, very slowly, raised his other foot, but instead of taking another step forward, he stepped diagonally sideways in a great stride – an exaggerated waltz movement – and once again he stood, frozen with obedience or indecision. The man's jerky, marionette-like movements had nothing to do with the quality of the film – obviously, he was in the grip of something he was powerless to control. It was almost uncanny, as if another independent entity was operating his limbs. In an earlier, more superstitious age, he might have been thought of as possessed by some unclean spirit.

During the Great War, the usual diagnosis for such behaviour was 'shell shock'. According to medical theory at the time, percussion waves from explosions rocked the skull, bruising or damaging the brain in some way, causing lesions, various kinds of mental conditions and aberrant behaviour.

I watched the man's agonisingly interrupted walk – even in its random path, there seemed to be a sustained intention – and then I understood. In a flash of recognition, I knew what was going through his mind. In some invisible terrain of the past – in some part of memory over which he seemed to have no conscious control – the man was walking across a minefield.

Once one has walked across an unmapped minefield, a walk in the country is never quite the same again. The ground – the humble surface one has trusted since childhood – has subtly changed its nature. Earth and dust have lost their innocence – the menace they might have concealed can never entirely be forgotten.

During the night, we often walked in single file along a trail. If there were mines, one man walked in front for as long as he was prepared to lead the way – then he fell back, and the next man would take his place. No one said anything. Some men went on for longer than others. Apart from the sick and the laggards, almost everyone took their turn at the front.

At the back of the column, the pace was slower and uneven – there was time to hesitate, and time to remember the possibility of seismic mines with delayed fuses, calculated to trigger at intervals along a length of trail for maximum casualties. Around well-known crossing points there were sometimes other, smaller mines, not much bigger than a pack of cards, scattered here and there. These smaller mines could blow off a foot or a leg, and were meant to slow a force of men while they tended the wounded – or at least wear down morale.

Lingering at the back was risky. One didn't want to lose contact with the main body of men. The iron rule was clear and had no exception: the group didn't wait for anyone. At the front, the momentum of the group following close behind made it easier to keep the pace – there wasn't any time to think, there was no choice – forward, inshallah!

The man in the grainy film, prancing around like a demented ballet dancer, was lost in a minefield. His movements were a perfect interpretation of the conflicting emotions when entering terrain where there might be mines – reluctance, determination, hope, fear, momentary terror, fatalism. In its way, it was an extraordinary performance.

At the end of the documentary, there was a public service announcement. Anyone who thought they might have been affected by issues raised in the programme could contact a helpline.

Had I been affected? I thought of the man, all those years ago, trapped in some unmapped landscape of the mind. At least by now his nightmare must be over.

But the image of the man skipping about like a puppet wouldn't go away. Slightly to my surprise, I picked up the phone and dialled the number on the screen. A warm, grandmotherly voice answered.

'Hallo dear, what can I do for you?'

The kindly question took me aback – what was I hoping for? What could this well-intentioned stranger do for me? How could she help me? The questions multiplied.

I must have paused a little too long because I heard the lady's voice again.

'Never mind, dear. Let's start with your name. Could you give me your name, please?'

My name. I'm reluctant to give her my name – it's not that I mistrust her, but the question raises other questions. Which name? My first name or my second name? My name here – the name on my passport – or my name over there?

I'm in that other territory, now. Careful. Measure the words to the face – otherwise, say nothing. Better safe than sorry.

'Hallo? Is anyone there?'

In a moment of painful clarity, I see how far there is to go – a far greater distance than I could have imagined – and I don't know if I have the strength. I haven't even begun.

It's dusk, and a barren grey expanse of rocks and sand stretches before us towards the horizon. Somewhere in the gathering darkness, there is a track and we must follow it towards the vanishing ghost of the setting sun.

'Hallo?'

The voice is gentle, but far away. I can hear the note of friendly concern, but by now I'm much farther away than I can explain to the old lady waiting for me to answer – in another place, in another time. It seems pointless trying – it would take too long, and there's so little time. Why begin?

'Hallo?'

The phone's in my hand, and I look at it.

'Hallo?'

The voice is even fainter now. I'm rarely lost for words, but now they're absent. No words. No name. Nothing.

A jolt of dumb emotion hits me so I can hardly breathe. Then, from nowhere, comes grief without words – shock at my inability to even say my own name – a blank sorrow for all that happened in the past.

My silence is unwilled – even so, I know what's going to happen next and I just have time to watch my hand replace the phone before the tears in my eyes cloud everything. This is the moment I know there's a problem – not a difficult problem, maybe, but something I don't understand – an unseen obstacle that gets in the way of what I'm doing, or trying to do.

Before, I had a vague sense of something in the background, now I'm sure. Thanks to the documentary, I can put a name to it – post-traumatic stress disorder – usually shortened to PTSD. The realisation is like a liberation. Oddly, I feel less alone knowing others have been where I am now.

The fifth of November – mulled wine at the local vicarage – and I'm with a Sunday school teacher who's talking about multi-faith awareness. I drain the last drops of sweet, tepid wine and look around for a refill. The rain's dripping from the lime trees and lighting the fireworks is getting tricky. Nearby, the vicar's silhouette is hunched over a smouldering cone – through the patter of raindrops, a muffled swear word – then a dollop of steaming wine pours into my paper cup.

A Roman candle softly belches a series of red, green and blue stars, then there's a hissing from somewhere in the darkness.

CRACK!

Soft ground.

CRACK!

Wet leaves.

CRACK!

'Are you all right?'

I look up at the man bending over me – the Sunday school teacher is anxious.

'What happened? Are you okay?'

I struggle clumsily to my feet. The paper cup's still in my hand, crushed and empty, and my wrist is drenched with hot, sticky liquid. He looks at the cup and gives me an almost sympathetic smile.

'Would you like another drink?' Somehow the intonation of the question suggests I might have had enough mulled wine.

'Wet leaves,' I say, 'incredibly slippery.'

'Yes.'

For a second, I consider a more detailed explanation, but I'm still trying to figure out what happened. A firework – a jumping jack or a crackerjack – and the next moment I hit the ground. Not for the first time, I'm confronted by a part of me that's insubordinate to my ordinary will. Something happens – a casual event unlocks a hidden force – leaving the conscious mind racing to catch up. Inwardly, I feel a flicker of unease. Who is this other that inhabits me? This aspect of my nature that moves faster than I can think – what is it? And what else might it do?

The Sunday school teacher's still standing there, looking at me with a glassy smile. Perhaps I'm imagining things – drunk, sick or crazy – it doesn't matter. I raise my crumpled cup, and give him my best imitation of a smile.

'Time for another.' The Sunday school teacher nods.

'It's good stuff,' I add – just for the hell of it, ramming the point home – and then I turn again towards the scent of cloves and cinnamon, beckoning in the dark.

It's summer in England, and the fields and hedgerows are silent in the heat. I'm walking along a footpath that follows a slow-moving river, I come to a bridge and pause for a few moments in the shade, watching sinuous bands of sunlight rippling and reflecting on the underside of the bridge.

A sudden metallic roar hits me – fear loosens my legs so they're like water – and I almost slip into the river.

A train going over a bridge – the noise overhead, like the thunder of a gunship – beside an English river. I'm still shaking as the sound of the train disappears in the distance, and the summer's warmth reasserts its drowsy peace.

The *Times* asked me to be bureau chief in Tokyo. I was away for a year or so, and it was hard. I missed my young son and his mother – we tried to talk on the phone almost every day, but it wasn't the same – and when I got back home it was different. Words – arguments – and tantrums so terrible they shook me to the core. I'd never experienced such violent anger from another person. My hands trembled and I became clumsy – loading the dishwasher, I dropped and smashed three glasses in as many days. After each eruption it took several hours to recover equilibrium – writing was almost impossible.

Was the problem with her, or me? Or was it her problem with me? The arguments were numbingly repetitive, always spiralling in towards one point – her *idée fixe* – the question that was really an accusation.

'When are you going to go out and get a proper job?'

Eventually, I said I was ready to leave, but she asked me to stay – so I did. I didn't want to go, but it was becoming a mad existence.

I loved my son – I loved his mother, too – but her rages were tearing everything apart. I would have liked to talk about the documentary with her, or the fireworks at the vicarage, but somehow it didn't happen. With everything else that was going on, there wasn't a chance of talking about the other strange dimension behind the facade of daily life – the peripheral sense of impending doom, like thunder on the horizon, or the sound of helicopters in the distance – an uneasiness shading into fear.

First the helicopters, then the bombing. The helicopters are looking for vehicles, and concentrations of men and animals – it's bazaar day, and people have come into town from the surrounding country. As the helicopters get closer, everyone – men, women, children – start running in all directions.

Panic.

It wasn't the sort of thing one could talk about – just like that – with anyone. With other men it could be tricky – just mentioning the war seemed to make some people uncomfortable. Maybe, secretly, they felt a touch of embarrassment not to have been there, or maybe it was guilt. Or envy. Or boredom. Women were more receptive, but most were parents and war isn't the chirpiest topic of conversation at the school gate. The ones who were single, understandably, had other priorities. With the few men and women who were there during the war, a rough-and-ready *esprit de corps* made talking about the odd memory – jitters, or jumpiness – seem trivial and unimportant. The military types didn't have much time for intellectualising, anyway – action was more their game – and no one in the army has any time for a whinger. It wasn't a matter of grin and bear it – nothing that bad – nor 'a Scout smiles and whistles under all difficulties', whatever that might mean. The jaunty ordinariness of some special service types seemed a good enough way of dealing with the blues. Or one could make do with the even-toned observation of a mucker from my days in Peshawar.

'Stuff happens – if you don't like it, don't think about it.'

Simple.

Easy to say, hard to do.

We shared a landscape – some of us even knew the same mountains, caves and valleys. We also shared a knowledge of another shadowy place, where images of the past remained – like primitive relics of another world – silent reminders of the best and worst of human nature. One could go there, if one wanted, but what was the point? It was all in the past, and too much trouble. Leave the shadows in the dark, where they're invisible.

There may be virtue in silence. ■

MATTHEW WELTON

Eight pieces in imitation of Thomas A. Clark

an infinite future
of hatchlings, buds, saplings –
the footpaths, mulch, pebbles
of the infinite past

=

the coherence of cloud
the fluency of wind
the articulation
of a chaffinch's song

=

the movements of still things –
streams, soil, ferns in the breeze;
the stillness of moving things –
falling leaves, clouds, hours

=

where the slope of the hill
grows suddenly gradual –
where the slope of the hill
grows suddenly acute

the green leaves on the branch
the dead leaves on the ground
the dead leaves on the branch
the green leaves on the ground

=

vertical trees along
horizontal footpaths –
their trunks in the sunlight
their trunks in the shadow

=

what it is about the stream
that the earth won't absorb it –
what it is about the earth
that it won't absorb the stream

=

the aptness of the air
to the buzzing of flies –
the aptness of the flies
to the buzzing of air

David Rakoff, 1964–2012

A PLAY ON MOTHERING

David Rakoff

The day after my brother Cameron reappeared in town and called me for the first time in six years, I went into my boss Caroline's office to tell her I needed some time off. I closed the door and explained things to her.

'Oh, Alexandra,' she sighed, playing her fingers lightly over her collarbones and bugging her eyes, as if she'd just run three miles or I'd crept up and frightened her. 'I thought you were coming in to tell me you were getting married!'

I do not have a boyfriend.

These are the rifts that one expects to read about in Hollywood biographies; children of the same great star but with different fathers who do not hear from one another in six years. In the movie version they're played by actresses of different nationalities, even.

The day I heard my brother Cameron's voice on my phone say my name, 'Alexandra?', I realized that I had let six years pass without having made any concerted effort to find him, and that I had been waiting for his call for just that long. Years ago, when my mother decided that she no longer had the energy to visit Cameron whenever he surfaced long enough to be admitted, I vowed that I would never submit to the weary, battered defeat she seemed to suffer. I would remain steadfast. This is not what happened, of course. I, too, became sickened and exhausted. Tired of seeing Cam in filthy clothes talking nonsense, or worse, screaming at me with unbridled rage and sex on his tongue. And when Cameron finally disappeared from town six years ago, where to I do not know, I felt nothing but relief for the first two years he was gone. I am not very adept at admitting my mistakes, and despite everything that has changed my feelings about Cameron, I have never called my mother to apologize. The subject of Cameron rarely comes up when we talk. When he had his first episode, I had followed her around the house, reading stentoriously from the pamphlets given to us by the psychiatrist (I mistakenly called them 'brochures', as if schizophrenia were a place with an exotic and vaguely medical reputation; the spas at Baden-Baden or the mud baths at the Dead Sea).

'Schizophrenics and those with schizo-affective disorders may experience a fractured and, to their minds, enhanced understanding of the world. Words, images, even objects are endowed with meanings unseen by the non-schizophrenic. For example, the word "psychiatry" may sound like "sigh Kaya tree", which may well bring to mind the image of a mystical plant to the schizophrenic. It is important,' and here my voice always rose in indignation, 'that the schizophrenic patient not feel his or her observations are being dismissed or ignored. Suggestions and pronouncements should be listened to and gently, yet firmly, denied.'

My mother wheeled on me. 'Alexandra. What would you have me do? Tell me and I will do it, I swear. Was it wrong of me to stop Cam from beating Bridget to death? When you have children, you can let them kill each other. I just hope I'm not around to witness it.'

This usually silenced me. The actuality of Cam's attack on my sister, her resultant and many years-long timidity and withdrawal, was something that excluded me, affording me only the most supporting role in the family drama.

'Cameron keeps on referring to a friend of his named Dorcas. I've checked with his teachers and there's no one at his school with that name. Is there someone here with that name? Is that a Greek name? Is it even a boy's name?' My mother's voice trailed off and she smiled apologetically at the doctor.

'There's no Dorcas here,' said the psychiatrist. 'What does Cameron say about this Dorcas.'

I rolled my eyes in embarrassment as my mother began to try to repeat what Cameron said. I could hear her calling up all her theatrical training when she spoke in Cameron's voice to the doctor. I felt that she was trying to give the doctor information and impress him with her mimicry in dangerously unbalanced proportions. And I felt that she was selling Cameron out with her, albeit skillful, imitation as a means of flirting with the doctor.

'Just tell him in your voice,' I hissed at her, barely able to cap my rage. 'This is not The Musicale.'

The tradition of the family musicale was around from the time we were very small. I was six or so, Bridget only about four and Cam a baby when it started because I remember my mother carried him in her arms when we first walked through the laneway in the back of our street banging on pots at midday, proclaiming, 'Come one, come all, to our living room, where we will present a play on mothering!' A few neighborhood mothers came, bringing their small children. My mother prepared inappropriately fancy food – red onion, cream cheese and caviar sandwiches on thin black bread, iced rosehip tea – and we performed our little play on mothering, all composed by our mother. It was titled 'Love and Individuality', or something similarly oblique. My mother put on one of her kimonos and was the mother bird, or deer, or lioness. Shot by a hunter, she collapsed on the living-room floor in a pool of plum-colored silk while Bridget and I, her small fledglings, now orphans in the storm, knelt over her, mewling in grief, clinging to one another for warmth in a cold world. Mother rose then, resurrected and transfigured by filial love. The end.

After some very perplexed and scattered applause, the mothers ushered their children politely and purposefully out the door, using no sudden movements, like they were dealing with a seemingly friendly yet huge and possibly erratic dog.

'What an interesting life you all lead,' said one mother, still holding her sandwich in the palm of her hand like a small jade mouse.

'Thank you so very much,' said my mother. These extra words were part of her Grande Dame mode of speech. 'You are kind,' she said, emphasizing the 'are' as if all the neighbors thought otherwise, and enfolded us into her huge sleeves. 'They do give me no small amount of pride.'

It never occurred to us to be embarrassed by the musicales, not for years. The little afternoon presentations continued. My mother performed the most unspeakably self-indulgent numbers – eyes half-closed as she turned around in slow, lazy, samba-like circles, her arms in the air over her head, humming to our Antônio Carlos Jobim record – 'an improvisatory variation on samba' she called it, or improvising tunes on the spot to Ogden Nash poems she read directly from the book. Bridget, Cam and I sat off to the side of the living room, quiet, not even looking, unfazed, waiting our turns. Some women came for years, after a while even abandoning the pretence of bringing their children, long after it was clear that my mother was both nuts and a not very good performer. They came because it beat doing nothing. They came for the sandwiches. In the evenings, when my father was still around, he would return to the house, his pinstripe suit at stark odds with us, still in costumes and makeup. He would eye the scattered platters and empty glasses.

'Ah, another salon, my dear?' he would ask wearily. 'Gertrude and Alice over again? Did Juan Gris get terribly drunk?' Then he would go off to bed.

All this continued every two months or so, until the time Cameron at age nine took out his penis and waggled it back and forth in front of the little girls in the neighborhood as part of his act. That ended The Musicale for us, and signaled Cam's high spirits as perhaps something more.

'Jesus, Cameron.' I say into the phone. I pause to take a drag on my cigarette.

'Yeah.' He laughs, pleased. Like his presence on the other end of my phone is some great trick.

'How are things?'

'Good. I'm back in town.'

'Yes, I figured, Cam. What for to do?' I can hear my voice encased in the smoothest ice. I am talking like our mother after a performance. Extra words out of order. If he tries to get at me, he will just slide off.

'Yeah, umm, there's a Korean-style bakery. Do you know?'

'No, what Korean bakery, Cam?' I pick a fleck of tobacco from my lip. My eyes are tearing up. I am the one who is sliding off. ('Hi, it's Cameron. I'm in town. I've met a wonderful girl and I just finished law school. I'd love you to meet her. She's named Irene.'

'Cameron, that's wonderful! I'm so glad you're feeling better.' This is what they don't tell you at the beginning when your seventeen-year-old brother has been admitted for having tried to pour gasoline on and light afire your twenty-year-old sister: this is forever. There is no scabbing over of this cut. It will ruin all your good clothes. It oozes and oozes.)

I ask it, against my better judgment. 'Cameron, would you like to come over?'

After I have given him my address and directions on how to get here. I call Bridget, whom I speak to virtually every day, although she doesn't live in town.

'Guess who's just called me.'

'Someone famous? Someone I know?'

We play twenty questions until she is stumped.

'Wrong,' I say. 'Cameron.'

'No shit,' she whistles. 'I really never would have guessed.'

This is one difference between me and Bridget. If someone were to walk up to me and hold out both fists and say 'Guess', I would say 'Cameron'. Then again, he didn't attack me.

'Does he even know where you live? Have you spoken to Ma?'

'No. I don't think I want to be part of that particular play on smothering.'

'I'll be honest with you, Allie. I actually thought Cameron would be dead by now,' Bridget says. 'Or maybe I just hoped so.'

There is a father and son trying to fly a kite at the other end of the football field. When we arrive, Cam stops and watches their halting progress, rapt. He grunts softly each time the boy throws the kite up as the father runs quickly. The kite nosedives immediately and knifes down to the ground. Eventually I say, softly, 'Cameron? Shall we walk?'

'Oh yeah, sure, sure.' He waves away the silly notion of the father and son with his hand and we walk to the center of the field. I find some hard candies in my pocket, probably from some restaurant, and hand him one. We sit down on the grass.

'Isn't this nice,' I say. Cameron has pushed the candy between his closed teeth and his parted lips and is sucking air and saliva through in a bubbling, slurping kind of way.

'It looks like the sky's keyhole now.' And I turn to look at the small distant kite and, indeed, he is right. It is a black punch-out against the horizon. I turn back to him to tell him how apt I think he is. He has made his hands into a clamshell, fused at the wrists. Smiling, he slowly opens the top half, making a creaking sound with his voice. The dome of the sky unlocked, lifting off. His hands are a jewel box and I lean forward and peer in, expecting maybe to find a ring. ■

A PLAY ON DAVID RAKOFF

A.M. Homes

His obituary described him as mordant and neurotic. I never thought of him as either – he was an inexorable blend of high and low; outraged and enthralled; rapt in wonder and horror. David found the humor in the tragic, and the tragedy in the banal. He was rare and singular; a Canadian and later an American citizen, a big Jew (his own term) and a gay man.

We became friends in New York in our early years out of college. We were all writing and working in publishing and he had a crush on a close friend of mine. What cemented our friendship was a particular night, a publishing party for young writers and editors on the far Upper West Side, a part of Manhattan that felt exotic and quasi-dangerous to me, who lived downtown in the West Village. As I write this I imagine a party not in the mid-1980s but in the late 50s or early 60s – I think of Truman Capote and Patricia Highsmith. Somehow that's how I saw us, or how it seems in retrospect: long, long ago.

The far Upper West Side was so far that we drove; I had a brown Honda Civic. When we arrived and everyone climbed out, I managed to lock my keys in the car. The others went up to the party but David, ever gallant, said he'd wait with me until the locksmith came. There were no cell phones, so we had to run up and down the stairs – no elevator – calling the locksmith, again and again. We stood outside in the Manhattan night; we leaned against the car; we sat on the hood; we sat on a stoop; and on the curb . . . We talked, and as we talked, things shifted and we began to sing Joni Mitchell, the album *Blue*: 'All I really really want to do . . . '

We sang the whole album – ten songs in order, a cappella, just two voices in the night. We missed the entire party, but we sang and as we sang we fell in love – the kind of love that can only happen when you're locked out, when you're singing Joni Mitchell late into the night with someone who knows it and feels it as you do: what it is to be an outsider, an alien, an artist struggling to articulate . . .

A t that point David had already had cancer once. He often made a point of telling me how he'd frozen his sperm. I like the idea that somewhere on ice there are still thousands of little Davids that could be unleashed and that if all his female friends – and there are many – were impregnated by this secret supply a whole generation of thinkers, humorists, novelists and artists would be born, a second generation of that unique Rakoffian sensibility. David's ability to hit a line, to pause, to take pleasure in whatever he was about to say – while at the same time laughing at himself – was so cutting and cute, and so irrepressible.

He was deeply grateful for all that he had in his life, particularly the love of his family and friends. I'm not sure if it's true, but I heard that his last words, spoken to his sister, were – *thank you.*

'Hey blue, there is a song for you.' Here is a song from me to you, David. I miss you. ∎

Demolition of an Armenian church, Bucharest, December 1986.

BUCHAREST,
BROKEN CITY

Philip Ó Ceallaigh

W hen his spirits were low, Romanian dictator Nicolae Ceauşescu would visit his fellow tyrants. A trip to Pyongyang – so the story goes – inspired him to bulldoze his capital. Between 1984 and 1989 a third of the old city, an area of some six square kilometres, was destroyed, and 57,000 families were relocated.

The centrepiece of the rebuilding effort was the presidential palace, the House of the People. Today, the House dominates the fractured detritus of downtown Bucharest. It is the seat of the post-Communist legislature and has been renamed the Palace of Parliament. The building remains mostly empty.

When I first settled in Bucharest, I lived in a depressed neighbourhood on the periphery. But the city centre, within view of the House, was worse. It felt like looking inside a madman's head. I never wanted to live in that razed and rebuilt area, but I have, since 2009. One evening I was drinking in a bar and offered to walk a girl home. I spent the night and never left.

U ntil the twentieth century, Bucharest's urban development was unplanned. 'Oriental' and 'Byzantine' were the words often used by visitors. Most of Ceauşescu's demolition took place along a five-kilometre east–west axis. The Boulevard of the Victory of Socialism

– the driveway for the House of the People – was built on the ruins of the old city. It is just over three kilometres long, eight lanes wide, is lined with apartment blocks and has been renamed Unification Boulevard, though it shears the city in two.

My home, in Strada Negru Vodă, is about two hundred metres north of the boulevard. The residential blocks here and throughout the reconstructed area were built for Party members. The apartments are more spacious than those in the brutally utilitarian socialist blocks elsewhere in Bucharest. The exteriors feature crude decorative features in unpainted concrete – bizarre pseudo-pillars, alarming zigzags and squiggles. Structurally, these buildings will resist a serious earthquake, but the facades have not aged well. Chunks regularly detach and crash onto the street below; handwritten signs warning you to mind your head appear after the fact.

Today, Strada Negru Vodă is the route for trucks supplying a mall. The street to the north goes to a Carrefour supermarket and its multi-storey car park. The pavements in this 'residential' area are occupied by parked cars, so pedestrians must walk on the road. By contrast, much of the area to the east has remained empty since the demolitions; a series of vast parking lots.

My home is comfortable, central, well heated and earthquake-proof. But my neighbourhood has no name. I tell people I live in one of the streets behind the mall.

An alley runs behind my block. Its far side is formed of the backs of the buildings of the next street. These are old; two hundred metres of one side of the street somehow escaped destruction. This strip of buildings gives an idea of the area's pre-demolition architectural mix: town houses with wrought-iron balconies from the end of the 1800s and art deco buildings from the 1930s.

Each month, I go to the administrator's office on the top floor of my block to pay for the utilities. From there, you can see the Star of David on the roof of the synagogue behind us. It dates from 1851, and is now the city's Jewish Museum; my neighbourhood was once at the heart of Bucharest's Jewish quarter.

The museum contains relics of hundreds of years of Jewish-Romanian life. The exhibit I like best is an 1871 map of the area that shows naively drawn churches, synagogues and other significant buildings in the streetscape. I find the street where the museum stands – Strada Mămulari. A little to the north of Mămulari were Strada Palestina, Strada Sinagogi and Strada Israelita: streets that no longer exist.

Continuity in place names can be misleading. My own Strada Negru Vodă is situated in the approximate location of the old Negru Vodă, a serpentine street that passed through a square and had roads and alleys spinning off it. One of those streets – now rubble beneath Carrefour's car park – was Strada Spaniola. A Sephardic synagogue called the Great Spanish Temple, dating from 1819, once stood on the old Negru Vodă.

In the Jewish Museum there is a copy, dated 1734, of Rabbi Benjamin of Tudela's *Voyages*. This twelfth-century travel journal mentions the presence of Jews among the Vlachs of the lower Danube basin.

It is useless to talk of 'first arrivals' or 'original inhabitants' in this area where people have always mixed. The Wallachian principalities were part of the Byzantine and then Ottoman worlds, if never fully incorporated politically. With the expulsion of non-Christians from Iberia in 1492, Sephardic Jews sought refuge in the Ottoman Empire and formed the first community of Bucharest Jews. Their language was Ladino, or Judaeo-Spanish. The development of commerce and towns in the Balkans is linked to the influx of the traders and craftsmen of the Ottoman Empire – Greeks, Armenians and Jews.

Bucharest was also on the fringes of the Habsburg and Russian Empires, and the decline of Ottoman power in the nineteenth century coincided with increasing trade with the north and west. By the 1800s, Yiddish-speaking Ashkenazi had become the larger Jewish community. The streets around my home were the meeting point between the Sephardic and Ashkenazi worlds; the place where these divergent strands of Judaism met again and mingled, with Romanian as their common tongue.

Only slowly have I learned of this neighbourhood that was lost beneath new buildings, car parks and wasteland three decades ago. It was five years before I even learned its name.

It was called Văcăreşti.

The writer Isac Peltz (1899–1980) had been a regular worshipper at the Avram Berl Zissu Synagogue, on the now-demolished north side of Strada Mămulari. His most famous novel was *Calea Văcăreşti*, published in 1933.

'I was born here,' said Peltz, in a 1979 interview. 'I lived among the book's characters. I knew their aspirations, victories, defeats, joys and sorrows. I am a child of the Jewish street. I started by sketching the portrait of several acquaintances, people of all kinds; pedlars, Yiddish actors, matchmakers, commercial clerks, shopkeepers, craftsmen with and without their own workshops, tailors, seamstresses, hairdressers, waiters, horse drivers, hotel porters, proletarians . . . I filled hundreds of pages with sequences from the tumultuous life of the old Bucharest ghetto.'

Learning about Peltz and reading *Calea Văcăreşti* – a collage of characters and incidents – I was curious to find out where the actual Calea Văcăreşti had run. Right by my door, as it turned out, though I needed a pre-1986 map to discover it.

For nearly five years I had been living on the ruins of Văcăreşti. The original inhabitants have died or been dispersed, and those who can remember Văcăreşti do not use the name to refer to the strange landscape that has supplanted it. When I came across the name 'Văcăreşti' in older writings, I had not known what part of the city it referred to.

Peltz lived long enough to see the world of his youth vanish but at the time of his death in 1980 he probably assumed that Calea Văcăreşti itself would endure, and that the title *Calea Văcăreşti* would continue to resonate with later generations of readers. My own copy of *Calea Văcărești* is from 1970, retrieved from a second-hand bookshop. Isac Peltz is now a forgotten writer, and Calea Văcărești a forgotten street.

I am looking at a black-and-white photograph showing Strada Mămulari, with the synagogue that is today the Jewish Museum, in an open field of frozen mud and snow. It is February 1986 and everything around this remnant street has been demolished. In the foreground, two excavators are at rest.

The photograph was taken by the architect Andrei Pandele, and appeared in his 2007 book *Photographs and Images, Forbidden and Personal*. I meet Pandele on the *terasa* of a restaurant just outside the zone of destruction, on a warm afternoon in autumn.

'Cities in Germany were carpet-bombed,' he tells me. 'Cities in Poland were flattened both by aerial bombardment and heavy street fighting. But Bucharest is the only city in Europe to have been destroyed in peacetime. This process had begun even before Ceaușescu dreamed up the House of the People. But what accelerated it was the earthquake that hit Bucharest on 4 March 1977.'

The minute-long quake measured 7.3 on the Richter scale. Ceaușescu was on a state visit to Nigeria and was unable to get a telephone connection to Romania for several hours. According to one story, he thought there had been a coup. According to another, he believed the whole city had been flattened. The damage he found once he returned to Bucharest the next day was bad enough: nearly 1,500 people had died, and many important buildings in the centre of the city had entirely collapsed.

Shortly afterwards, Ceaușescu demanded proposals from a number of notable architects for a new earthquake-proof presidential palace, which would later be called the House of the People. He was informed that the safest place in Bucharest to build was the Hill of the Arsenal, next to the ancient monastery of Mihai Vodă, above a labyrinth of streets in the oldest part of town.

From the outset, Ceauşescu envisioned a giant building. Competition between architects ensured that he was soon offered something many times larger. Then, when construction was under way, he demanded that it be expanded even further.

In 1987, Andrei Pandele was dispatched to work on the House of the People after a conflict with his superiors at the Institute of Architecture. He became one of the four hundred architects responsible for the finishings and finer details of the structure. He was therefore able to enter the area around the Boulevard of the Victory of Socialism at a time when it was off-limits to the general population – the presence of a scattering of guards with Kalashnikovs was enough to deter anybody not on legitimate business. Pandele often took his camera along – he was an accredited photographer for a sports newspaper, which provided a legitimate reason for carrying one, should he be stopped by the police – and documented the demolition and subsequent construction of the House. Any one of these pictures, if discovered, would have resulted in a prison sentence. Just as risky were his photographs of food queues, factory life and the aftermath of the 1977 earthquake. You have to wonder too at his nerve of photographing Mikhail Gorbachev's cavalcade during the Soviet leader's May 1987 visit to Bucharest.

In public places, Pandele rarely had the luxury of lifting the camera to his eye and composing a shot. He would dissimulate by looking in one direction and – hand casually resting on the camera hanging against his chest – shoot in another. 'It was very hit-and-miss. I ended up with a lot of worthless shots. Many were out of focus. And the shutter made a clunky sound, so I needed the cover of machinery or other noise if there were other people around.'

He minimised the danger by not keeping prints of his work. 'I'd make test prints on paper, to see what I had, but I'd destroy them. The negatives I stashed at my in-laws' home. I thought that maybe in twenty years Ceauşescu would be dead and Nicu [his son] would declare that his father had gone too far, and I'd be able to take the photos out.'

After the revolution – he photographed that too – Pandele realised that the thousands of images he had accumulated constituted an unparalleled visual archive of life under Communism in Romania, and of the city before and during demolition. But his books weren't published until 2007.

'I was unable to do anything with the photographs in the 1990s,' he explains. 'The images were too raw, too ugly. People didn't want to look in the mirror. What they saw disgusted them.'

Văcăreşti was never exclusively Jewish. The part closest to the city centre contained a number of important civic buildings and old churches, including the Church of Sfânta Vineri, which stood some two hundred metres to the north of my home, where Calea Văcăreşti began.

On 13 June 1987, Elena Ceauşescu, the wife of the dictator, stopped to inspect Sfânta Vineri, and declared to her entourage: 'Away with this rubbish.' The parish priest, Father Gelu Bogdan, was initially told that only the annexes would be demolished, and the church grounds expropriated. By 19 June, as the bulldozers arrived, it became clear that the church itself would not survive. Sfânta Vineri had a reputation as a philanthropic institution and was popular with poorer parishioners. Even after so much of the city had already been destroyed, the demolition of this ancient church was significant. When the demolition of the annexes to the church began, a crowd began to gather. By the afternoon there were an estimated 2,500 people there, and around six o'clock the police created a cordon and pushed people back. But the workers refused to raze the church, and neither would the soldiers. Prisoners were brought in to do it, in return for shorter sentences.

One eyewitness I talked to, Horea Murgu, arrived as two bulldozers commenced their work. People watched in resignation, some in tears. In the evening, parishioners laid candles on the footpath and in the rubble. There was some subdued prayer and singing, under the gaze of the security forces.

The Church authorities made no attempt to mobilise the thousands of people who had gathered to watch the demolition, and always avoided direct confrontation with the regime. The patriarch of the Romanian Orthodox Church was visiting Vienna that day. It is hard to know whether his absence was more convenient for the regime or for the Church.

Another witness to the demolition was Andrei Pandele. The pictures he took that day are, to my knowledge, the only ones that exist of the event.

One photograph shows several bulldozers beginning to dismantle the church. The crowd is gathered in the foreground across the street, faced by one soldier. Pandele shot the image from behind, at a slight elevation. The onlookers all face away from him. The only exception is a man in the bottom right of the frame. He is looking straight at the photographer – straight at *me*, as I examine the photograph – and frowning. It is perhaps a coincidence, but you could never tell who was Securitate, or an informer.

Today a monument commemorates the church on a large traffic island looped by tramlines. A thick concrete wall rises from ground level to a height of over two metres, covered with lightweight marble tiles of the kind you might see in a service-station bathroom. In the wall is a cruciform gap, big enough to step through. Most of the aluminium sheeting that originally plated the top of the wall has been stolen for its scrap value. The wall itself is defaced by graffiti and posters advertising a variety of services. Thousands of people pass here daily, crossing the street between bus and tram stops, or heading down to the mall, the supermarkets and the metro station. I am sure very few of them know what the monument represents, or read the inscription on the small cross stating that Sfânta Vineri was built in 1645 and demolished in 1987. This is a place where churches have dates of birth and death, like people, and where even monuments to destruction become part of the ruin.

'Many churches were destroyed and the Church was silent,' the writer Norman Manea tells me. From 1984 to 1986, Manea lived on the edge of the area of demolition and recalls the constant din of heavy machinery, day and night. 'This was not the Polish Church, which opposed the system on principle,' he says.

'The Orthodox Church had every reason to be an enemy of the system too, but the tradition of the Orthodox Church is to be extremely obedient, whether to the king or whoever happens to be in power. The files uncovered after '89 show, I think, that more than half the priests were informers. So this is already scandalous. Because those who go to the priest go for advice, for something that will ease their situation – if everything they say goes directly to the secret police, the nightmare is perfect.'

Manea, who is Jewish, left Romania in 1986 under pressure of increasing Securitate harassment and a climate of what he describes as 'a delirious anti-Semitic campaign in the official nationalist press'. He now spends most of his time in New York.

'The Jews had an option, in that they could leave,' continues Manea. 'Most of my family left. Some immediately after the war, some a little later. The tendency to leave became stronger with the years. The Jewish community as an institution, like the Church, also played a very ambiguous role at that time, in that they had a kind of complicity with the system. But they had a goal, which was to convince the authorities to let the Jews go. So this may excuse some not very pure or honest things they did from the political point of view. The very shrewd chief rabbi of the time succeeded in getting the Jews away from Romania and directing the greatest part of them to Israel. This was in itself a great achievement for that time. It didn't happen in other socialist countries.'

Manea describes leaving Romania in 1984 as his *second* exile. The first was in 1941, at the age of five, when he was deported with his family and the entire Jewish population of the eastern and northern regions of Romania to an area of Ukraine administered by Romania's wartime fascist regime, headed by Marshal Ion Antonescu. An estimated 100,000 of the deportees never returned. They were shot, or died of starvation and disease. Manea returned in 1945, along with the surviving members of his family.

In the summer of 1942, arrangements were made for the deportation of Jews from Bucharest and the south of Romania to a concentration camp in Poland. The plan was never implemented, even though Adolf Eichmann, the logician of the final solution, had set about obtaining the necessary rail stock for the operation. The Romanian authorities had discovered that the Jews they were about to hand over to the Germans for free could be sold for $1,300 a head for emigration to Palestine. Then, as the Red Army got closer to Romania, the regime decided it was good policy to let its Jews go, free of charge.

The trade in Romanian Jews that began during the Holocaust continued virtually uninterrupted until the overthrow of Ceauşescu. In the early Communist period, emigration was permitted in exchange for economic aid from Israel. By 1969 – in addition to the economic assistance – Ceauşescu was charging for each Jew permitted to leave, starting at $2,000 and rising to $25,000 for doctors and scientists. By 1987, there were only 23,000 Jews left in all Romania. Today there are perhaps 10,000.

From the 1960s onwards, the regime became increasingly nationalistic; no discussion was permitted of anything that might complicate the narrative of Romanian national destiny. During the quarter-century of Ceauşescu's rule, the Holocaust was not denied as such, it was simply not talked about. After the collapse of socialism, the nationalist residue remained in the public discourse. In the 1990s, history in Romanian school and university books ended with the outbreak of war in 1941. Awareness of the Romanian Holocaust began with an official state acknowledgement in 2004, three years before the country joined the EU, as a result of external pressure.

Out of the fifty-five synagogues that existed in Bucharest before the war, only two remain as places of worship. One of these is the Great Synagogue, the last of the active Văcăreşti synagogues. It was built in 1847 by Ashkenazi Jews and was once known as the Polish Synagogue. It was badly vandalised in the 1941 pogrom. Today it is hidden behind a horseshoe of modern blocks, accessible only from the rear, across a mix of wasteland and parking lots. It is also Romania's Holocaust Museum; during services, curtains are drawn over the exhibits arranged around the inside walls. Its devotional use is temporary; it is substituting for the Choral Temple, which is under renovation.

Written in relief on the facade of number 12, Strada Olteni – so faded as to be almost invisible – is the name of the architect, one M. IANCU.

Marcel Iancu – Janco, outside of Romania – founded the Dadaist movement with fellow Romanian artist Tristan Tzara in Switzerland during the First World War. A painter, designer, architect and social theorist, Iancu saw art as a tool for social progress, along with improvements in education and advances in technology and medicine. He designed forty buildings, erected in Bucharest in the interwar period. In 1935, the year the Strada Olteni block was completed, Iancu published a Le Corbusier-inspired manifesto in a book titled *Towards an Architecture for Bucharest*. 'For Bucharest, the chance will not come again,' he wrote.

The modern style demands modern town planning. This is the hour of decision for the structure, basic geometry and lines of continuity for Bucharest's urban development . . . A remade Bucharest will in fifty years be happy and healthy, a garden city, a place of parks and palaces . . . Town planning is the art we must use to look into the future. Those who build cities without sufficient foresight always end up overwhelmed by reality.

Iancu's manifesto resounds with the modernist faith in progress and enlightened central planning.

In 1980, towards the end of his life, Iancu wrote: 'Born as I was in beautiful Romania, into a family of well-to-do people, I had the fortune of being educated in a climate of freedom and spiritual enlightenment.' But by 1938, anti-Semitic legislation had put an end to Iancu's career in his native city. He emigrated with his family to British Palestine in February 1941, a month after a pogrom devastated Văcăreşti and left over a hundred people dead. One of the victims was Iancu's brother-in-law, Misu Goldschlager, who was kidnapped from his home and killed in an abattoir. Goldschlager and the fourteen other victims, some of them children, were hung on meat hooks. Many of the corpses were eviscerated; others had signs with the word 'kosher' attached to their corpses. Testimony by a secretary to a government minister at the time suggests that the victims were tortured and hung on meat hooks while still alive.

Marcel Iancu died in Israel in 1984.

The systemisation of Bucharest's streets and the architectural standardisation which gives the city its present visual character was well advanced before the 1977 earthquake struck. New neighbourhoods of ten-storey blocks had gone up all around the city on what was previously countryside and on the main roads radiating from the centre. The gentle sprawl and oriental disorder of Bucharest's streetscape was brusquely overlaid with high-density housing and almost identical boulevards and this modernist reconstruction of the city in the seventies created the momentum for the destruction of the centre in the 1980s.

From the 1970s, much of the city had become a building site, and it was socialism itself that was under construction. The new housing imposed a new style of communal living, and absorbed a tide of immigration from the countryside. The newcomers were also the labour force for the work of demolition and construction. Between 1970 and 1989 the population of the city almost doubled. Transport infrastructure also expanded: during this period Bucharest's underground rail system was built.

Between 1984 and 1989, the city centre was a vast building site, employing, at its peak, 100,000 construction workers operating in shifts. Even as the people of Bucharest suffered cuts in electricity, water, gas and heating, the economy of the nation was focused on building. The terrible atmosphere of stagnation and hopelessness I remember in Bucharest for over a decade after the revolution is easily comprehensible in terms of how much construction work simply ceased to exist when the system commanding it collapsed.

Once, to give a foreign visitor a sense of the scale of Ceauşescu's project, I asked a taxi driver to take us down the Boulevard of the Victory of Socialism as far as the House of the People. The driver became an enthusiastic guide. He had himself worked on its construction. He recalled that it had been a good time and that the pay was decent. He was proud of the size of the House and was able to cite statistics about how many light bulbs the building used – its electrical consumption was equivalent to that of a small city.

There is madness in the House of the People, I have always felt. But I am a latecomer and my feelings are not always shared. Many of those who lived through this great experiment are loyal to the logic of socialism. For them, it was an era of dynamism. Here was a state that got things done, that drew up great plans and carried them out, and was decisive in a way a democracy – a corrupt democracy – is not.

Half a million people, brought to Bucharest, given jobs and homes and a project for the future, were bitterly let down by the revolution and the freedoms that came with it. They do not see the 'destruction' of Bucharest; they just see that the construction abruptly stopped.

The new National Library, on the boulevard of the Victory of Socialism, was one of Ceauşescu's flagship projects of civil architecture. It was uncompleted at the time of the revolution. No further significant work was done for over a decade, while traffic streamed down the Boulevard, past this monument to great intentions. It was only inaugurated in 2012, and even now feels disconnected from the city it presumes to serve. The area to the east has remained a wasteland for over a quarter century: a stadium-sized parcel of land that has been excavated to a depth of several metres below the level of the surrounding area. If you approach it through the scrub that separates it from the roadway, the desolate remains of concrete foundations become apparent. Calea Văcărești once ran diagonally across it.

And there I was, in the library, chatting to a journalist, with a view across the boulevard towards the blocks of my own neighbourhood on the other side. The room was terribly overheated but the din of traffic was too great for us to be able to open the windows. I gestured to the boulevard and the Communist blocks, and said something about the demolitions.

'Yes, this is one of the best areas in Bucharest for real-estate prices,' said the journalist, who I guessed was about twenty-five.

But didn't she think the destruction of the capital was criminal? Sometimes I have to remind myself that my interest in the recent history of my city is not shared by everybody and I try to control my voice when I make such suggestions.

Oh, it was very hard to say, replied the journalist. There were good things and bad things. She worked hard, but couldn't afford a trip out of the city. At least back then people could take holidays. Today there was so much poverty. That day she'd met an old woman begging at a bus stop. She showed me a picture she'd taken of her on her smartphone. I mentioned forced expulsions, bulldozers. Oh, she responded, it was very hard to know what was better. She was determined to be open-minded.

Only information of the hard sort has a chance of penetrating this kind of mental fog, and hard information is largely absent from the written record of the time. One exception is Saul Bellow's *The Dean's December*. Bellow had visited Bucharest late in 1978 – a year after the earthquake – with his Romanian-born wife, Alexandra Bagdasar, who was returning to see her dying mother. Bellow's Romanian translator, Antoaneta Ralian, describes finding Bellow shaken both by the oppressive atmosphere of a police state – his lodgings were bugged, the concierge reported to the Securitate, he was tailed in the street – and by commonplace hardships. Heating was almost non-existent, the water supply intermittent. In *The Dean's December*, Bellow described the city through the eyes of the fictional Albert Corde:

> December brown set in around three in the afternoon. By four it had climbed down the stucco of old walls, the grey of Communist residential blocks; brown dullness took over the pavements, and then came back again from the pavements more thickly and isolated the street lamps. But you were bugged in the flat . . . if you wanted to talk privately you went out . . . The flat was as tentatively heated as it was electrically dim . . . Aged women rose at four to stand in line for a few eggs . . . Corde had seen the shops and the produce, the gloomy queues – brown, grey, black, mud colours, and an atmosphere of compulsory exercise in the prison yard . . . On [TV] you saw nobody but the dictator. He inspected, reviewed, greeted, presided; and there were fanfares, flowers and limousines. People were shown applauding. But if emigration were permitted, the country would be empty in less than a month . . . It was one of the greatest achievements of communism to seal off so many millions of people . . . Of course, as in France under the Occupation, the captive millions were busy scrounging, keeping themselves alive . . . Clearly the guys in charge were psychopaths.

After its publication in English in 1982, Bellow's books disappeared from the shelves of bookshops and libraries in Romania.

Born of Russian-Jewish immigrants, Bellow had a peculiar perspective on the death of Europe, having first witnessed it in depression-era Chicago. He viewed the neighbourhoods of his youth as extensions of the old continent: fundamentally dynamic places despite their poverty that were animated by the skills of the craftsmen and traders of the cities of Europe. In the 1970s he wrote: 'The slums, as a friend of mine once observed, were ruined. He was not joking.' Bellow saw the city losing its European character in the second half of the twentieth century, under a tide of immigration from rural southern states, with workers drawn by the offer of assembly-line jobs. When heavy industry collapsed, these low-skilled workers became an underclass, inhabiting an impoverished inner city that was abandoned to violence, crime and drugs.

In Bucharest, in 1978, Bellow witnessed the ruin of Europe for the second time: a city destroyed by fascism and the Holocaust, and then by communism. Had he visited a few years later, when the demolitions had begun, he would have found an even more powerful image for the suicide of civilisation – another echo of blighted Chicago's 'endless square miles of ruin'.

What concerned Bellow, when he wrote *The Dean's December*, was how a polity, even a democratic one, could fail to direct itself consciously. For how else could a free society fall into a collective sleep deep enough that a great city would expire at its core?

And this is what I wonder about too. I am reminded that it is only consciousness and memory that hold together the things we sometimes see as solid.

I'm not a Jew or a Christian and I'm also not Hindu, but each week I visit a quiet apartment scented by sandalwood where I am instructed in Advaita Vedantic scripture by a Tamil Brahmin. I wash my feet before entering the room and sit cross-legged before my teacher, who speaks for up to an hour and a half. Sometimes, if there is time, he takes questions relating to the text being studied. My legs are always stiff at the end, and afterwards I go and have a beer or two on my own on my way home.

I dabble in the philosophy of detachment to calm down just enough to see how screwed up I am, then I head back into the world. I live in an apartment with a woman and a small child. I have to make money. Sometimes I can't sleep. Often I am so tired I can't connect the thought in my head to what I was thinking five seconds before.

I remember the architecture professor Sorin Vasilescu, who spoke at a public debate I attended about the destruction of the churches. He told us how shortly after the revolution he'd talk about what had happened to the city and the people who were forcibly moved, but now that so many years have passed he notices that his words no longer have the power to engender emotion. The world has moved on and fewer people can remember what the city was like or connect imaginatively with it. And if that is gone, he wondered, does this not mean that this connection with the past – this tradition – is broken irremediably? And should he, as a teacher, simply accept this?

I go to my own teacher, and he tells me that anxiety is the attempt to hold on to what is changing. We must identify those things that are subject to change, and hitch our wagon to the infinite.

I wasn't against my daughter being baptised but I wanted nothing to do with it either. Her mother took care of the arrangements. Most Orthodox priests in Bucharest charge for performing the sacrament and she had a problem with that so she found a priest who asked only for a donation to the church.

The Church of Bucur the Shepherd is reputed to be the oldest in the city. It is a tiny chapel, dating from the 1600s and built on the site of a church from the 1400s. That in turn, they say, was built on the site of an even earlier church, built by the legendary shepherd Bucur. Bucharest ('Bucureşti' in Romanian), so the story goes, was founded by this shepherd. The chapel is on a small hill, probably formed from the debris accumulated over centuries of habitation and successive rebuilding. The River Dâmboviţa flows by here, and the settlement may have arisen at a ford that was later bridged to allow the passage of flocks. Sheep were the basis of the economy of the region between the Danube and the Carpathians throughout the Middle Ages, and so the idea of a shepherd-founder may have some historical basis.

It was here that we gathered on a day in late October. We stood outside waiting for a previous baptism to finish and I was sorry I had not brought a coat. The weather had changed that day, and a cold wind was blowing. The tiny church is sandwiched between a Communist-era apartment block and a new concrete-and-glass corporate building, but it stands on the borderland of the destruction and is curiously exposed. Behind the chapel the ground falls away several metres, and this small cliff provides a viewing platform overlooking the empty plain where the city had been. I stood by the railings, looking out across a great distance towards the Boulevard of the Victory of Socialism. Across this wide emptiness the cold wind blew.

In the 1980s, the eastern slope of the mound had been cut away and the ground levelled as part of a project to straighten the course of the River Dâmboviţa and to hem it between concrete banks like a giant sewer. What was possibly the most important archaeological site in the city was excavated by bulldozers and whatever story the ground could have told was churned up and then encased beneath asphalt and cement.

It was our turn. My daughter's four grandparents were there and her two surviving great-grandparents had travelled from their village in Oltenia. The chants of the priest alternated with singing by three seminarians. My daughter was content, surrounded by people and music. Towards the end came the actual baptism – total immersion of the five-month-old child in a metal basin of tepid water, three times in rapid succession. When she came up the third time I expected her to scream, but she only looked extremely surprised. She was immediately wrapped in a towel and set down on a table to be dressed in new clothes, symbolising the new life. Until this point I had stood back from this ritual, but seeing my daughter still stunned from the dunking, I stepped forward, next to her. I thought she would like to see my face. Orthodox churches have no seating, except along the walls. They are fluid spaces in this sense, and the chapel was so tiny that it was only a few paces from the margins to the action. I stood beside her and she gripped my finger in her fist and they dressed her. I felt we had already known each other a very long time. And then she was dressed and we were already thinking of moving on, going to where we would sit and eat and drink for the rest of the day. The bearded Father wound things up by talking about the newly baptised, whom he judged to be a very confident sort of person, which struck me as a funny way to talk about a baby, but which also seemed true. He talked about her as though she was a soul who had come into this world complete, which was the way she seemed to me too, in the brief time I'd known her – that she was already made, revealing herself in her own way.

We set off, driving across the disrupted city on a windy autumn day, suddenly cold, the leaves about to be shaken from the trees, across the Boulevard of the Victory of Socialism, through the vacant spaces and past the blocks. Most of us had come to the city since it had been ripped apart and had never known it to be different, or else had been born too late, and it looked as it always had to us. We were doing what normal people do. We were living, not trying to remember back to before our time, to wars and earthquakes and madness. We went to where the food and drink were laid out and where the music played, north of the zone of destruction, where the city begins again. ■

GAZA, MODE D'EMPLOI

Eduardo Soteras Jalil

Same magazine, different format

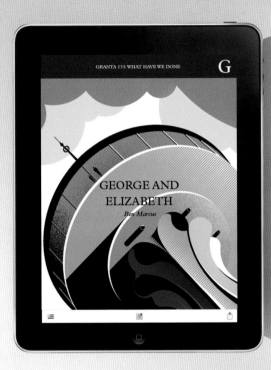

New app out now

GRANTA.COM

GRANTA

THE MAGAZINE OF NEW WRITING

PRINT SUBSCRIPTION REPLY FORM FOR UK, EUROPE
AND REST OF THE WORLD (includes digital and app access).
For digital-only subscriptions, please visit granta.com/subscriptions.

GUARANTEE: If I am ever dissatisfied with my *Granta* subscription, I will simply notify you, and you will send me a complete refund or credit my credit card, as applicable, for all un-mailed issues.

YOUR DETAILS

TITLE ....

NAME ....

ADDRESS ....

POSTCODE ....

EMAIL ....

☐ Please tick this box if you do not wish to receive special offers from *Granta*
☐ Please tick this box if you do not wish to receive offers from organisations selected by *Granta*

YOUR PAYMENT DETAILS

1) ☐ Pay £32 (saving £20) by direct debit

To pay by direct debit please complete the mandate and return to the address shown below.

2) Pay by cheque or credit/debit card. Please complete below:

1 year subscription: ☐ UK: £36   ☐ Europe: £42   ☐ Rest of World: £46

3 year subscription: ☐ UK: £99   ☐ Europe: £108   ☐ Rest of World: £126

I wish to pay by ☐ CHEQUE   ☐ CREDIT/DEBIT CARD

Cheque enclosed for £_____ made payable to *Granta*.

Please charge £ _____ to my: ☐ Visa ☐ MasterCard ☐ Amex ☐ Switch/Maestro

Card No. ☐☐☐☐☐☐☐☐☐☐☐☐☐☐☐☐

Valid from *(if applicable)* ☐☐ / ☐☐   Expiry Date ☐☐ / ☐☐   Issue No. ☐☐

Security No. ☐☐☐

SIGNATURE .... DATE ....

Instructions to your Bank or Building Society to pay by direct debit

BANK NAME ....

BANK ADDRESS ....

POSTCODE ....

ACCOUNT IN THE NAMES(S) OF: ....

SIGNED .... DATE ....

DIRECT Debit

Instructions to your Bank or Building Society: Please pay Granta Publications direct debits from the account detailed on this instruction subject to the safeguards assured by the direct debit guarantee. I understand that this instruction may remain with Granta and, if so, details will be passed electronically to my bank/building society. Banks and building societies may not accept direct debit instructions from some types of account.

Bank/building society account number

☐☐☐☐☐☐☐☐

Sort Code

☐☐ ☐☐ ☐☐

Originator's Identification

☐9☐ ☐1☐ ☐3☐ ☐1☐ ☐3☐ ☐3☐

Please mail this order form with payment instructions to:

Granta Publications
12 Addison Avenue
London, W11 4QR
Or call +44(0)208 955 7011 Or visit
GRANTA.COM/SUBSCRIPTIONS for details

© SUNRA THOMPSON

READING COMPREHENSION: TEXT NO. 2

Alejandro Zambra

TRANSLATED FROM THE SPANISH BY MEGAN McDOWELL

I suppose we were happy on my wedding day, though it's hard for me to imagine now. I can't quite fathom how, in an era of such bitterness, any sort of happiness was possible. This was September of 2000, fourteen years ago, which is a long time: one hundred and sixty-eight months, more than five thousand days.

The party was memorable, that's for sure, especially after that soulless, torturous ceremony in our apartment. We'd done a thorough cleaning the night before, but I think our relatives still whispered about us as they left, because there's no denying that those threadbare armchairs and the wine-stained walls and carpets didn't come together to give the impression of a place fit for a wedding.

The bride – of course I remember her name, though I think eventually I'll forget it: someday I will even forget her name – looked lovely, but my parents just couldn't understand why she would wear a black dress. I wore a gray suit so shiny and shabby that an uncle of the bride's said I looked more like an office gofer than a groom. It was a classist and stupid comment, but it was also true, because that was precisely the suit I'd worn when I worked as an office gofer. I still associate it, more than with the wedding, with those endless days I spent walking around downtown or waiting in line at some bank, my hair cut humiliatingly short and wearing a cornflower-blue tie that could never be loosened enough.

Luckily, the official from the civil registry left straight away, and after the champagne and modest hors d'oeuvres – I remember with shame that the potato chips were all crushed – we had a long lunch, and we even had time to take a nap and change our clothes before our friends began to arrive, bringing, as we'd requested, generous alcoholic contributions instead of gifts. There was so much booze that soon we were sure we wouldn't be able to drink it all, and because we were high, that seemed like a problem. We debated the issue for a long time, although (since we were high) maybe it wasn't really that long.

Then Farra carried in an enormous, empty twenty-five-liter drum – I don't know why he had it in his house – and we started to fill it up, emptying bottles in at random while we half-danced, half-shouted. It was a risky undertaking, but the concoction – that's what we called it, we thought the word was funny – turned out to be delectable. How I would love to go back to the year 2000 and record the exact combination that led to that unexpected and delicious drink. I'd like to know just how many bottles or boxes of red and how many of white went in, what was the dosage of pisco, of vodka, of whiskey, tequila, gin, whatever. I remember there was also Campari, anise, mint and gold liqueurs, some scoops of ice cream and even some powdered juice in that unrepeatable jug.

The next thing I remember is waking up stretched out in the living room, not just the bride and me but a ton of other people, some of whom I'd never even met, though I don't know if they were crashing the party or if they were distant cousins of the bride, who had – as I discovered that night – an astonishing number of distant cousins. It was maybe ten in the morning, we were all having trouble stringing words together, but I wanted to try out the ultra-modern coffee maker my sister had given us, so I brewed several liters of coffee and little by little we shook off our sleep. I went to the big bathroom – the little bathroom was covered in vomit – and saw my friend Maite sleeping in the tub, sprawled in an unlikely position, though she looked pretty comfortable, her right cheek pressed against the ceramic tile as if it were an enviable feather pillow. I woke her up and offered her a cup of coffee, but she went for a beer instead to keep the hangover at bay.

Later, at around one in the afternoon, Farra switched on a camera he'd brought to film the party but had only just remembered. I was flopped in a corner of the room, drinking my zillionth coffee while the bride dozed against my chest. 'How does it feel, man?' Farra questioned me, imitating the tone of an overenthusiastic small-town reporter.

'To be married?' I asked him.

'No: to be married in a country where you can't get divorced.' I told him not to be an ass, but he insisted. He told me his interest was genuine. I didn't want to look at him, but he went on filming me. 'Why celebrate so much,' he went on, relentlessly, 'when you're just going to separate in a couple of years? You'll call me yourself. You're going to come to my office desperate for me to process your annulment.'

'No,' I answered, uncomfortable.

Then the bride sat up and rubbed her immense green eyes, caressed my hair, smiled at Farra and said, lightly, as if she'd spent some time thinking about the matter, that as long as divorce wasn't legal in Chile, we wouldn't separate. And then I added, looking defiantly into the camera: 'We will stay married in protest, even if we hate each other.' She hugged me, we kissed, and she said that we wanted to go down in Chile's history, we wanted to be the first Chilean couple to get divorced. 'It's a stupendous law. We recommend that everyone get divorced now,' I said, playing along. And she, looking at the camera too, with unanimous laughter in the background, seconded the sentiment: 'Yes, it's an absolutely commendable law.'

'Chile is one of the few countries in the world where divorce isn't legal,' someone said.

'The only one,' someone else clarified.

'No, there are still a few,' said another.

'In Chile,' Farra said, 'the divorce law will never pass. They've been arguing over it for years and nothing's happened, with the whole rotten Catholic lobby against it. They even threatened to excommunicate any representatives on the right who voted for it. The world will go on laughing at us.' Someone said that the divorce law wasn't the most urgent thing to be fixed in the country, and then the sluggish conversation turned into a collective debate. As if we were filling up another drum, this time with our complaints or our wishes, almost all of us had something to contribute: the urgent thing is for Pinochet to go to jail, to go to trial, to go to hell; the urgent thing is to find the bodies of the disappeared; the urgent thing is education. The urgent thing is health care, said someone else, and then came another, others: the urgent thing is to fight capitalism; the urgent thing is for Colo-Colo to win the Copa Libertadores again; the urgent thing is to fuck over Opus Dei; the urgent thing is to kick Iván Moreira's ass. The urgent thing is the war on drugs, added one of the bride's distant cousins, getting everyone's attention, but right away he clarified that it was a joke.

'We live in the country of waiting,' the poet said then. There were several poets at the party, but he was the only one who deserved the title, because he tended to talk like a poet. More precisely, he spoke in the unmistakable tone of a drunk poet, of a drunk Chilean poet, of a young, drunk, Chilean poet: 'We live in the country of waiting, we live in wait for something. Chile is one giant waiting room, and we will all die waiting for our number to be called.'

'What number?' someone asked.

'The number they give you in waiting rooms, dumbass,' someone said. Then there was complete silence and I took the opportunity to close my eyes, but I opened them again right away, everything was spinning.

'Goddamn, you talk nice,' Maite told the poet, then: 'I could really be into you, if it weren't for how small your dick is.'

'And how do you know that?' asked the poet, and she confessed she had spent hours hidden in the bathtub, looking at the penises of the men who went to piss. The poet said, with a slight but convincing scientific intonation, that the size of the penis when pissing was not representative of the penis in an erect state, and there was a general murmur of approval.

'Let's see then, show it to me erect,' said Maite, all in.

'I can't,' said the poet. 'I'm too drunk to get it up. You can try going down on me if you want, but I'm sure I won't get hard.' They went to the bathroom or to the poet's house, I don't remember.

'I'm sorry,' Farra said to us later, I suppose regretfully, the camera turned off: 'I don't want you to separate. But if one day you do, you know you can count on me, both of you: I'll separate you for free.' I don't know if we smiled at him, now I think we did, but it must have been a bitter smile. The guests left one by one, and it was night by the time we were alone. We collapsed into bed and slept about twelve hours straight, our arms around each other. We always slept in an embrace. We loved each other, of course we did. We loved each other.

Two years later, just as Farra had predicted, we went to see him in his office. The divorce law was still stalled in Congress; it was said that its approval was imminent, but Farra told us that in no way was it worth waiting for. He even thought that afterward, once it passed, divorce would be more expensive than annulment. He explained the process to us: we'd already known that the judgment of nullity was ridiculous, but when we found out the details, it also struck us as immoral. We had to declare that neither she nor I had lived at the addresses that appeared on our marriage contract, and we had to find some witnesses who would attest to it.

'How idiotic,' I told the bride that afternoon, at a cafe on calle Agustinas: 'How pathetic, how shameful to be a judge who listens to someone lie and pretends not to know they're lying.'

'Chile is idiotic,' she said, and I think that was the last time the two of us were in total agreement. We didn't want to get an annulment, but it was fitting, in some sense. Now that I think about it, the best way to summarize our story together would be that I gradually annulled her and she me, until finally we were both entirely annulled.

In May 2004, Chile became the penultimate country in the world to legalize divorce, but the bride and I had already gotten an annulment. Maite and the poet, who by then were a couple, were going to be our witnesses, but at the last minute the poet backed out and I had to ask the favor of the woman whom, a few years later, I married. I'm not going to tell that story here; it's enough to say that with her, things were completely different. With her, things worked out: she and I were able, finally, to divorce.

EXERCISES:

1. The general tone of this story is:

a)   Melancholic
b)   Comic
c)   Parodic
d)   Sarcastic
e)   Nostalgic

2. What is the worst title for this story – the one that, it goes without saying, would appeal to the widest possible audience?

a)   'Five Thousand and One Nights'
b)   'Two Years of Solitude'
c)   'Fourteen Years of Solitude'
d)   'Two Weddings and No Funeral'
e)   'The Labyrinth of Nullity'

3. In your opinion, who are the victim and the victimizer, respectively, in this story?

a)   The bride / The groom
b)   The poet / Maite
c)   Chile / Chile
d)   Liver / Concoction
e)   Liquor / Beer

4. According to the text, at the beginning of the twenty-first century, the nation of Chile was:

a)   Conservative in its morality and liberal in its economy
b)   Conservative in its insobriety and artificial in all things holy
c)   Innovative in its levity and literal in its tragedy
d)   Aggressive in its religiosity and conjugal in its wizardry
e)   Exhaustive in its chicanery and indecisive in its celerity

5. The narrator doesn't mention the bride's name because:

a)   He wants to protect her. Moreover, he knows that he doesn't have the right to name her, to expose her. That fear of naming her, in any case, is so 90s.
b)   He wants to protect the woman's identity because he's afraid she might sue him.
c)   Although he says he will even forget her name, maybe he's already forgotten it. Or maybe he's still in love with her. He swears he no longer remembers her name, but he knows just what to call her: Maria.
d)   He's a no-good heartbreaker. He's a liar and a cheat. And a misogynist. And sexist.
e)   If you can't be with the one you love, love the one you're with.

6. According to the text, the divorce law wasn't passed earlier in Chile because:

a)   The Catholic Church lobbied intensely, even threatening to excommunicate the Congress people who supported the bill.

b)   There were other priorities in the areas of health, education and justice.

c)   The priority was to put off indefinitely any reform that might put the country's stability at risk.

d)   The priority was to put off indefinitely any reform that might put at risk the interests of corporations and the impunity of those responsible for crimes during the dictatorship, including, of course, Pinochet. In this context, the divorce law was hardly a question of values, and even the right-wing leaders – many of them 'annulled' and remarried – knew it was disgraceful that Chile still hadn't legalized divorce, but they put the matter off until they needed a powerful distraction that would neutralize the public outcry for justice and radical reforms.

e)   A much better system existed: annulment. Because when a couple separates, what we really want is to believe that we were never married, that the person with whom we wanted to share our lives never existed. Nullity was the best way to erase the un-erasable.

7. Which of the following famous phrases best reflects the meaning of the text?

a)   'Marriage is the chief cause of divorce.' (Groucho Marx)

b)   'Love opens the parentheses, marriage closes it.' (Victor Hugo)

c)   'A second marriage is the triumph of hope over experience.' (Samuel Johnson)

d)   'Unable to suppress love, the Church wanted at least to disinfect it, and it created marriage.' (Charles Baudelaire)

e)   'Marriage is the only adventure open to the cowardly.' (Voltaire)

8. The end of this story is, without a doubt:

i)   Sad
ii)   Heavy
iii)   Ironic
iv)   Abrupt
v)   Immoral
vi)   Realistic
vii)   Funny
viii)   Absurd
ix)   Implausible
x)   Legalistic
xi)   Bad
xii)   It's a happy ending, in a way

a)   i, ii and iv
b)   x
c)   All of the above
d)   viii and xi
e)   xii

LAST DAY ON EARTH

Eric Puchner

When I was young, seven or eight, one of my father's German short-haired pointers had puppies. These were marvelous things, trembly and small as guinea pigs and swimming all over each other so they were hard to count. Their eyes, still blind, were like little cuts. After a few days my father decided we needed to dock their tails. He shaved them with an electric razor, then sterilized some scissors and had me grip each puppy with two hands while he measured their tails and snipped them at the joint. It was horrible to watch. The puppies yelped once or twice and then went quiet in my arms, as still as death. I didn't want my father to see what a wimp I was, so I forced myself to watch each time, trying not to look at the half-tails lined up on the porch, red at one end so they looked like cigarettes.

When it was time to dock the last puppy's tail, my father handed me the scissors. It seemed important to him that I do it. *Don't think too much,* he told me. When it came time to snip, though, I couldn't stop thinking and did it too slowly and there was a sense of cutting through something strong, like rope, except it was tougher than rope and gave me a curled-up feeling in my stomach. The puppy began to yelp and thrash around and I made a mess of the thing, snipping several times without finding the joint so that my father had to cut the tail shorter than all the others. He was upset. These were expensive dogs, and you couldn't sell one that wasn't perfect. Still, my father loved me back then and didn't make a big deal of it; he was planning on keeping two of the pups anyway, so he named her Shorty. He could do that in those days – turn his disappointments into a joke.

During hunting season, my dad went shooting once or twice a month, squeezing Shorty and Ranger into the back seat of his Porsche and driving out to a game farm in Hampstead County. I used to get up at the crack of dawn to see him off. He must have known I liked helping him because he always asked me to carry something out to the car: his first aid kit or his decoys with their keels sticking down like ice skates or once even his Browning 12-gauge shotgun in its long-handled case. But it was his Stanley thermos that seemed magical to me because my father's breath, after he took a sip from it, would plume like smoke. My mother hated coffee – 'motor oil', she called it – and so I connected it with being a man. Often my dad didn't return until after dark, his trunk lined with pheasant, which he'd carry into the house by the feet. They looked long and priestly with their perfect white collars, red faces arrowed to the ground. It made me feel strange to look at them, and a little scared.

 After we moved out to California, my dad stopped hunting, which meant there was no reason to keep Shorty and Ranger in shape. They stayed in their pen all day, whimpering and getting fat. There was an old horse corral on the property we'd rented, and my dad had set up the pen inside it, which, despite the creeping shade of an avocado tree, meant the dogs spent much of the day in the hot sun, snapping at flies. The barn was a good ways from the house, and eventually I stopped really thinking about them. The whimpering made me sad for a while, and then it didn't. I was fifteen by then. My dad kept saying he was going to find a home for them, but then he moved out himself and left my mom to take care of us – me and the dogs.

 'We're going to the animal shelter,' my mom said one afternoon. She was sitting at the kitchen table, holding a glass of white wine. I'd never seen her have a glass of wine before six o'clock. I inspected the bottle on the counter – it was half-empty, sweating from being out of the fridge.

'What?'

'I told your father that if he didn't come get the dogs this morning, I was taking them to the shelter. I've been asking him for six months. It's past one and he isn't here.' My mother took a sip from the glass in her hand.

'They'll put them to sleep,' I said.

'You don't know that for sure.'

'No one's going to adopt some old hunting dogs. How long do they try before giving up?'

'Seventy-two hours.' My mom looked at me, her eyes damp and swollen. 'Your father won't deal with them. What am I supposed to do?'

My mother couldn't even get rid of a spider without ferrying it outdoors on a piece of paper. Then again, the dogs were unhappy, perhaps sick, and I certainly wasn't going to be the one who got up at six in the morning to run them up and down the driveway. I had no interest in dogs or hunting. The only time I ever got up early in summer was to go surfing, and I groused so much anyway that my friends usually regretted taking me.

My mother poured herself another glass of wine, which spilled when she lifted it. She'd begun to wear contact lenses again, something she hadn't done in a long time, and her eyes looked naked and adrift without her glasses. On the kitchen counter was a book called *Unlocking the Soul's Purpose*. I wished my sister were here to see her – my mom, drunk and strange-eyed in the kitchen – but she lived in Africa, doing something for the Peace Corps I hadn't bothered to understand. She was nine years older, too worried about puff adders hiding in her shoes to care much about our parents' troubles.

I handed my mom a dish towel. 'Dad's going to go apeshit,' I said, hoping the swearing might upset her.

'Ha. Believe me. That doesn't even begin to describe it.'

'Maybe he's tied up at work,' I said.

'Your father doesn't have a job, remember?'

'He's starting his own business.'

My mother laughed. 'With his girlfriend?'

'It's a savings and loan,' I said, ignoring this.

'Caleb,' my mother said. 'He's two million dollars in debt.'

I smiled at her. 'That's money he's *invested*,' I said patiently. 'Venture capital.'

My mother got up to put her glass in the sink. My dad had told me all this a couple weeks ago, the last time we talked on the phone, but it was just like my mother not to understand. 'Your mother's an idiot,' my father said when I told him she'd described him as 'unemployed', and what shocked me more than the word itself was how sincere he was – how calmly diagnostic, as if he were trying to make sense of his own hatred. As soon as he said it, I had a feeling like when you drink a Coke too fast and burp it into your head. There was something about her, something needy and timorous and duty-bound, and it had driven my dad away. And now he would be furious about Shorty and Ranger – furious at me, too, for failing to stop her.

When they realized they were going in the car, Shorty and Ranger skittered around the driveway before hopping into the back seat. It made me both happy and sad to see they could still muster some excitement. My mother shut the door quickly, as if she couldn't bear to look them in the eye, and I remembered that she was the one who'd always groomed and bathed them when my dad wasn't running them up and down the yard, talking to them in a dopey, dog-brain voice that occasionally made me jealous. 'Buster,' she called Ranger sometimes, which is what she also called me, at least when I was little.

'We should do something for them,' I said, 'before we take them to the shelter.' I needed time to think.

'Good idea,' my mom said, looking relieved. 'Where's the happiest place for a dog?'

'The beach?'

She smiled. 'Of course. The beach. My God, I don't think they've ever been.'

I climbed into the front seat while my mother shut up the pen. The dogs watched me eagerly from the back seat. Shorty's muzzle, I noticed for the first time, had begun to go gray. 'You're not going to die,' I told them, though they didn't seem worried. Already a plan had begun to take root in my brain. My mother, trying to unhook the orange whistle from the door of the pen, dropped it in the dirt.

'Do you need me to drive?' I asked her when she got in the car.

'Don't be ridiculous. You haven't even finished driver's ed.'

She managed to back the Mercedes successfully down the dirt road, even with the FOR SALE sign covering half of the rear window. My mother did not have a job – hadn't, in fact, graduated from college because she'd become pregnant with my sister – and despite my efforts at denial the new reality of our lives was beginning to sink in. Selling the Mercedes was not going to be enough to support us. The house had a tennis court and a swimming pool overlooking the canyon, and though I didn't know how much the rent was, I knew it was much more than we could afford. We'd given notice for the end of the month, but only now, watching my drunk mother back out into the street, did it occur to me she had no idea what we were going to do.

But I wasn't too worried. Not because I had any sentimental illusions about my parents getting back together. They hated each other, that was clear, and I was happy that no more dinners were going to be ruined because of it, my mother locking herself in her room to cry. My father wasn't going to leave me high and dry, though. He'd told me as much after the separation. He'd take me in, if I wanted, just as soon as he found a bigger place. He was looking in Corona del Mar, trying to find a house on the beach. I could surf every morning if I wanted to. The name itself – Corona del Mar – sounded like a foreign country to me, a place you sailed to in a dream. Very soon he'd zoom up our driveway in his Porsche, bearing pictures of our new house, grinning in the way he used to when the trunk was full of birds.

At Grunion Beach my mother opened the glove box and fished
out her old sunglasses. They were white and mirrored and
hopelessly out of style, the kind you saw on the ski slopes with little
leather side-shields on them.

'How do I look?' she asked me.

Poor, I wanted to say. I pretended to drink the coffee I'd made
her buy me at 7-Eleven. It tasted terrible, but I didn't care. I liked
the warmth of it in my hand. We let the dogs out of the car, and
they ran down the dusty trail before splashing into the water and
then galumphing back out when a wave caught them. This was
not the beach where I surfed. Homeless people came here, and
spear-fishermen in scuba gear, and strange, well-dressed men with
briefcases who looked like they'd walked through a mirror in London
or Hong Kong and ended up at the beach by mistake.

It had taken some sly work to steer my mother here, and now I
told her I had to use the bathroom. Instead I headed for the payphone
and called my father, my heart stamping in my chest. I'd never been
there, to my dad's apartment, but I knew the address from all the
letters my mom had to forward – *Now I'm his collection agent, too* – and
I pictured the phone ringing just a mile or so up the street, wondering
if his girlfriend would answer. I'd tried sometimes to imagine what
she looked like: tall-booted and glamorous and at home in the front
seat of a Porsche, the opposite of my mother in every way.

When the machine came on and my father's voice asked me to
leave a message, I was almost relieved. I explained what was going on,
that he needed to come find us as soon as he could.

'Mom wants to murder Shorty and Ranger,' I told his answering
machine.

Down on the beach, my mother was absorbed in her Slurpee,
sucking on the straw with her eyes closed. I'd been astonished to see
her buy anything for herself at 7-Eleven, let alone a Slurpee, which
she used to say would 'rot my liver'. Shorty and Ranger sniffed
around for dead things, looking happier than I'd seen them in a long
time. It was a beautiful afternoon – sunny and cool, with a breeze like

a can of perfect ocean smell – and it was hard to imagine anything being killed.

'I haven't been to the beach in years,' my mom said. She slipped off her sandals and dug her feet into the sand, and you could see the warmth of it spread across her face. Her sunglasses, when she tipped her head back, looked like a piece of the sky. 'Believe it or not, we used to have a great time together. You and me. Ocean City, remember? We used to bury each other in the sand, like mummies. Your sister too. Even your father got a kick out of it.' She shook her head, as if the fact that we didn't go to the beach together anymore was my fault. 'I should have come down here more often.'

'You still can,' I said. 'You can come here whenever you want.'

She looked at me. 'Do you really believe that?'

'Why not?'

'That I can skip down to the beach whenever I want, just for the hell of it?' She seemed angry, though it was hard to take her seriously with the Slurpee in her hand. 'Nice try, but I'm going to have to get a job.'

I smiled. 'Like what?'

My mother lifted her ridiculous sunglasses. 'You don't think I have any skills or talents?'

I shrugged. No, I didn't really think she did. She had an okay singing voice, nothing to write home about, and sometimes she could solve math problems without a calculator – but I couldn't really think of anything else, anything special about her.

'I see,' she said, slipping her sunglasses back on. Her lips, damp from the Slurpee, looked thin. She gazed down the beach, where Shorty and Ranger were sniffing at a giant bullwhip of kelp. 'Remember when your father made you dock Shorty's tail?'

'Not really,' I lied.

'I was glad you couldn't do it,' she said, ignoring me. 'It gave me hope for you.'

I took another sip of coffee. The taste almost made me gag, but I decided right then to force myself to like it. Shorty and Ranger looked up from the kelp they were sniffing, distracted by a guy scanning the beach with a metal detector. He was wearing those stupid headphones that beachcombers wear, moving his machine back and forth like a blind person's cane, so tan it was hard to make out his face. He waved at us, smiling, and my mom tugged the hem of her dress over her knees. I had never talked to a beachcomber before and lumped them in the same category as men who collected lost balls from the gully near the golf course, folks my dad called 'bottom feeders'. I hoped Shorty and Ranger might scare him off, but the man walked up to them boldly and let them sniff his hand.

'Fine dogs,' he said to me, taking off his headphones.

He was wearing a madras shirt unbuttoned at the chest, exposing a tussock of gray hairs. I'd heard the term 'salt-and-pepper mustache' before, but this was the first time I'd seen one in real life. In another context – if he had been holding a tennis racket, say, instead of a machine for grubbing up lost change – you might even have called him handsome.

'German shorthairs?'

I nodded.

'Did you raise them yourself?'

'They're my father's,' I said.

'Used to have a GSP myself. Frisky, her name was. She had hip dysplasia, so the name was perhaps ill-chosen.' The man glanced at my mother, and I had the feeling that he was speaking to her somehow and not me, the way you might try to speak to a ventriloquist by talking to his dummy. He looked down the beach. 'Where's your paterfamilias, if you don't mind my asking?'

'My what?'

'Your father.'

I glanced up at the parking lot. 'I don't know.'

The man nodded, as if turning this over in his mind. He waved the detector in our direction, and it beeped so loudly that Ranger barked. 'Sorry,' he said, frowning. 'Are you wearing a ring?'

My mother shook her head.

'It's attracted to you nonetheless.'

She blushed. The man asked if we had a spot of water on us – 'feeling a bit sponged out here today' – and astonishingly my mom lifted her Slurpee and offered him a drink. His mustache, when he handed the cup back to her, was red.

My mom laughed. She lifted her sunglasses again and perched them on her forehead. How different she looked without them: tired and sun-stamped, the corners of her eyes mapped with little lines. She was forty-five. Something in the man's face seemed to relax.

'We don't want to interrupt your beach hunting,' I said.

'Not at all. I was just going to take a little breather.' My mom sucked noisily at her straw, and the fact that she wasn't completely herself – that she was a bit drunk – seemed to dawn on him for the first time. 'It's me, possibly, who's interrupting something?'

'Caleb was just discussing my talents,' my mother said, narrowing her eyes. 'Namely, how I don't have any.'

The man regarded me gravely. The idea of her talentlessness seemed to offend his cosmic sense of justice. 'Nonsense. Everyone has a God-given talent.'

'Well, He skipped me. Didn't He, Caleb? I'm pretty much useless.' My mom smiled at me, but there was a hardness to her eyes that I'd only ever seen directed at my father.

'I don't believe you,' the man said. 'Not for one second.' He looked at me, then back at my mother, as if trying to figure out what he'd walked into. 'You mean to tell me there's *nothing* you've ever done that made people go: "Hello, look at her, I'm impressed"?'

My mother cocked her head. 'In college, I could walk on my hands,' she said finally. 'At parties they'd chant: "*JP, JP*"– that was my nickname – and I'd walk around like that. Once I even walked to class that way, just for kicks.'

'There you go,' the man said, vindicated.

I looked at my mother. I knew for a fact that she couldn't walk on her hands. She couldn't even keep up with her exercise video, *Aerobics for Beginners*. I had never heard her lie before, about anything, and it gave me an ugly feeling.

My mother glanced at the sieve hanging from the man's belt. 'And your talent, I gather, is finding hidden treasure?'

'I have a certain knack,' the man said, and winked at her in a way I didn't like.

'How does that thingamajig work?'

The man unstrapped his arm from the machine, which looked like one of those crutches old people wear except with a wire vining up the shaft to a fancy-looking control box, and handed the contraption to my mother. Then he slipped the sunglasses gently from her head and pinched the headphones over her ears and positioned himself behind her, gripping her hand with his own, leaning in to her as if he were teaching her to hit a golf ball. The man showed her how to sweep the coil over the sand, back and forth. My mother laughed at something, and there was a look on her face I hadn't seen in a very long time, not since my parents used to get dressed up for parties and my father would tell her, in a voice I didn't recognize, how 'radiant' she looked. She smiled as the man showed her how to work the knobs and buttons, asking him to repeat himself for no reason. She seemed to hang on every word. Though I had the sense, too, that she was trying to prove something to me, that the real her had stepped out of her body like the angel in a cartoon and was watching me the whole time. I looked away. Shorty and Ranger were panting in the sand, exhausted from chasing waves, and I felt suddenly short of breath, too, and a little sick, as though I might throw up. A tire squeaked in the parking lot – my heart leaped – but it was just a lost Jeep turning around. Where the hell was he?

When I turned back to my mother, the beachcomber was still gripping her hand. She caught my eye suddenly and stepped away. Her dress was rumpled. She took off the headphones and handed the metal detector back to the beachcomber.

'How much does it cost?' she asked politely.

'Seven hundred,' he boasted. 'You can get cheaper ones, but not with a zero-to-ninety-nine target ID.'

'What a rip,' I said.

The man turned to me and frowned, studying me for a second. 'Tell that to the guy who found the Mojave Nugget.'

'The what?' my mom asked.

'Mojave Nugget. 4.9 kilos of solid gold.' The man hitched up his pants. 'You wouldn't believe the treasures lurking underfoot. Friend of mine, just last week, found a diamond ring, and no river rock either. One and a half carats.'

I snorted.

'Pardon me?' the man said.

'Mojave Nugget. Jesus Christ. Don't be a moron.'

'Caleb!' my mother gasped.

'Will you please just go look for pirate treasure somewhere else?'

The man seemed about to speak, to put me in my place, but my face seemed to make him reconsider. He straightened his shoulders. Gallantly, he handed my mother her sunglasses and then started back toward the water before stopping a few feet away to slip his headphones on, as if to show everything was fine. My mother wouldn't look at me; she put her sunglasses back on and plopped down in the sand again.

'Does it feel as good as you thought it would?' she asked after a while.

'What?'

'Calling someone an idiot.'

I nodded, though it didn't feel good at all. My mother busied herself with her feet, swishing sand over them until they disappeared. I'd never heard her sound so disgusted with me. She yawned, and the disgust in her face seemed to shrink back into sadness.

'Okay, Buster,' she said to Ranger, checking her watch.

I glanced at the parking lot. 'It's only three o'clock.'

My mother stared at her missing feet, then at me. I remembered burying her in the sand in Ocean City, how my sister and I would cross her arms over her chest like a pharaoh's. It seemed like something from a different life.

'Here,' I said, kneeling beside my mother and beginning to dig a trough.

'What are you doing?'

'Burying you in the sand.'

My mother yawned again. 'God, I'm so tired,' she said. 'Must be the wine. I feel like I could sleep right here.'

I dug with two hands. The idea was to keep us here till my father showed up – keep us here, at least, until I could get ahold of him. The sand was less hot the deeper I plowed, each layer cooler than the one above it, and the coolness under my fingernails versus the warmth against my wrists was such a specific, one-of-a-kind sensation that I came unstuck from time for a second. I could half-hear the shrieks of Ocean City, half-smell the whiff of my mother's sun lotion, half-see the smile on my father's face as he smeared the lotion into her back and made her hum like a girl. His wet hair was swooped back and perfectly parted – he carried a folding comb, one that popped out like a switchblade, even to the beach – and I found him incredibly dashing. One time, walking back to the car on the hard part of the beach where the surf had retreated, he stopped to show my sister and me the print of his sneaker tread in the sand, a perfect impression, complex as a tiny fortress. Embossed in the middle of it was the word SADIDA. My father found this to be a marvelous thing. *Sadida*, I said to myself, because it sounded strange and marvelous to me too. And then my mother made a shoe print next to my father's – she was wearing sneakers as well, her old Tretorns – and we stopped to admire this too, the four of us laughing for no reason, and I remember making the long drive back to Baltimore, feeling bored and lucky and spanked all over from the sun, and thinking *Sadida Sadida Sadida* as we chattered over the Botts' dots on the highway.

Now my mother lay down in the trough I'd dug, looking up at me in her sunglasses, and I started to push sand over her legs and arms and torso. I buried her as best I could. Shorty and Ranger watched me work. When I was done, she was a mound of sand with a head sticking out. Her cheeks, like mine, were dusted with freckles.

I let her lie there in her sunglasses, tucked to her chin, until I wondered if she'd fallen asleep. 'Mom,' I said, but she didn't answer.

Then I jogged up the path to the parking lot, Shorty and Ranger trailing behind me as if I were leading them to the next great happiness. They waited by the phone as I rummaged in my pockets. I had another quarter, I was sure of it, but all I could find was a dime and a nickel. I checked the change slot: empty. I was fifteen years old – practically a man, or so I believed – but I felt suddenly like I might cry. I don't believe in psychic powers or anything like that, so I can't explain the certainty I had that afternoon, staring at the rusty phone and its rain-warped Yellow Pages dangling from a cord: a feeling beyond all doubt that my father was home, that he'd been there all day, that he was busy working and hadn't gotten my message.

I peered over the rocky berm to where I'd left my mother on the beach, but couldn't see her face. She was just a lump of sand. The beachcomber, too, was nowhere to be seen. I felt as strange as I've ever felt.

I checked under the rear fender of the Mercedes and found the little magnetic box where my mom kept a spare set of keys and loaded Shorty and Ranger into the back seat before climbing behind the wheel, blinded by the leathery heat. There was a map in the glove compartment, tearing along the folds. I looked up my dad's street. The Mercedes started right up, no problem, and though I lurched a bit in reverse, I managed to get out of the parking space well enough and coax it onto the road. I spaced my hands at nine and three o'clock on the wheel, as I'd been taught to do. The big car seemed to glide along, responding to my thoughts. I'd dreamed about it so often that it was like I'd been doing it for years. I pulled onto Palos Verdes Drive North, making sure to keep a three-second space cushion between me and the car ahead. I couldn't help thinking how easy – almost disappointingly natural – it was, this adult thing that all my life had seemed like magic.

I found my dad's street and turned down it, bucking over a speed bump that sent Shorty and Ranger tumbling from the back seat. At first I thought I had the wrong address. I'd been expecting a condo complex, but this was a stucco apartment building shaped like a box and propped up on stilts. It looked like it might try to creep away in the middle of the night. 'Saxon Arms' was written on the front in medieval-looking script. Parked under the building, squeezed between two of the stilts, was my father's Porsche.

I let the dogs out of the back seat and we walked around to the other side of the building, their collars jingling, and climbed the stairs. One of the apartments had a BEWARE OF DOG sign, emblazoned with the picture of a snarling pit bull, taped inside the window. I stopped at my dad's door and knocked. It was not a long flight of stairs, but my heart was going as if I'd run all the way from the beach.

'Caleb!' my dad said when he saw me, nearly dropping the CD in his hand. He was wearing sweatpants and one of those pleated Cuban shirts with tiny buttons where there weren't any buttonholes, which I'd never seen him wear before. He hugged me in the doorway, and I could smell the coffee on his breath mixed with the chemical newness of his shirt. Music played behind him; he was a jazz fan – Fats Waller, that old stuff – and I realized how much I missed hearing its delirious ruckus around the house. Shorty and Ranger barked, excited to see him, and my father bent down to say hello, closing the door most of the way behind him.

'Did you get my message?' I asked.

'I did,' he said, glancing behind him. 'Just now. I've been on my office phone all morning.' He cleared his throat. 'Wow. Look at you. How the hell did you get here?'

'I drove.'

'You have your license already?'

I nodded. My father eyed me carefully – suspiciously, I thought – and then treated me to the rare abracadabra of his smile. 'Serena's taking a shower. She's been lying out on the patio. The woman can sunbathe through an earthquake.'

The idea of her lying out in the middle of a Tuesday, instead of dealing with bills or laundry or groceries, seemed exotic to me. Scattered on the welcome mat was a pair of pink flip-flops. My dad bent down to collect them, grumbling under his breath, and Ranger slipped into the apartment. 'Ranger, heel!' my father said, jogging after him. Shorty and I followed into what looked like the living room, though it was hard to say since the only furniture was a futon folded up into a pillowless couch. Nearby, tucked into one corner, was a kitchen area with a little stove and a microwave whose door was open and some *Vogue* magazines stacked on the counter next to a Carl's Jr. bag. One of the cupboards had the sticker of a Teenage Mutant Ninja Turtle on it. I searched around for the office he was talking about.

'I've got my eye now on a house in Manhattan Beach,' he said without looking at me. He grabbed Ranger's collar and pulled him away from a ficus plant in the corner, glancing at the closed door beyond the kitchen. I could hear pipes moaning inside the walls.

'What about Corona del Mar?'

'It's like Club Med down there now. Anyway, those cliffs? Whole town's sliding into the ocean.'

My father turned down the music, then glanced again at the closed door of the bedroom. He hadn't thanked me for bringing Shorty and Ranger, but I chalked this up to my appearing out of the blue. Shorty found the Carl's Jr. bag on the counter and tried to pull it onto the floor, pawing her way up the cupboard.

'Down, girl!' my father said and yanked Shorty's collar, hard enough that she yelped. The dog skidded over to me, crouched on her hind legs. 'No one cleans up around here. It's dog heaven. Didn't you bring their leashes?'

'I thought you'd want to save them from the shelter.'

'I do, Bud. I do.' My dad's face softened. 'But they're pointers. I can't keep them cooped up in here. They're run-and-gun dogs.'

'Mom's going to kill them.'

'It's me she wants to kill,' he said proudly. He looked at Shorty and then glanced away again, as if he couldn't meet her eye. 'Does she talk about me?'

'Mom?'

'We lived in an apartment about this size, in New York. This was before your sister was born. The boiler didn't work right, or maybe the landlord was just a prick, but we could see our breath in that place. Your mother stole some bricks from a construction site – a pregnant woman! – and heated them in the oven. We slept with hot bricks at our feet.'

'Can't you keep them for a little while?' I said. 'Till the house is ready?'

'I wish I could, Bud, but they're not allowed in the building. Not even shih-tzus. It's in the lease.'

The pipes in the wall squeaked off, and my dad excused himself and disappeared into the bedroom. I could hear him talking to his girlfriend behind the door, the muffled sound of their voices – I imagined her naked from the shower, dripping all over the carpet – and after a while I had the ghostly sensation, watching the dogs sniff around the kitchen, that we weren't in my dad's apartment at all. From outside drifted the sounds of a nearby pool, the echoey shrieks and splashes, and I thought about when Shorty and Ranger were puppies, soon after my father had docked their tails, how he'd trained them to swim. We'd had a swimming pool in Baltimore and I remembered how he'd waded into the shallow end with them one at a time, cradling them in one hand and then lowering them into the pool that way, holding them until they got used to the water. They looked small as rats to me, their tiny heads poking above the surface. My father had them swim to me as I knelt on the deck – how scared I was that they'd drown! – but they made it to me eventually, trembling as if they'd just got back from the moon, and my father took them again and whispered something in their ears, clutching them preciously in both hands.

Eventually, my dad emerged from the bedroom with his girlfriend, who was fully dressed and drying her hair with a towel. She was pudgier than my mother, and not as tall, and had one of those dark tans like she'd stepped out of a TV set that had the contrast knob turned all the way to the left. She'd done up her shirt wrong, and I could see her belly button, deep as a bullet wound, peeking between buttons. She hugged me with one arm.

'I've heard so much about you,' she said nervously, then laughed. She stepped back from me. 'God, listen to me. That's just what I'm supposed to say, isn't it?' She noticed the dogs and went over to say hello to them, squatting down so they could sniff her hand. She scratched Ranger affectionately, just above the tail, and his hind leg began to bounce. 'Ah-ha. The way to every dog's heart.'

My dad frowned at her, trying to send her a message across the room, but she didn't seem to notice.

'I thought they'd be more ferocious,' she said.

My father snorted.

'Don't they kill birds?'

'Right,' my father said. He smirked at me. 'They have these little dog guns, and they shoot them out of the sky.'

His girlfriend bristled. 'How am I supposed to know? I grew up in Burbank.'

She went out to the porch to hang her towel on the railing, and I heard a dog bark in a neighboring apartment. The one with the sign in the window, it sounded like. Shorty and Ranger began to bark as well. My father glanced at me, then cocked his head toward his girlfriend and gave me a secret look. He'd always been a mystery to me, a man of ingenious surprises, but now I knew exactly what he was going to do: roll his eyes. And that's precisely what he did. He rolled his eyes, one man to another, the only people in the world with half a brain.

At the beach, I parked the Mercedes and headed down to the water, Shorty and Ranger jingling behind me. I was jingling too, my mom's keys in my pocket. The three of us jingled down the path.

My mother was right where I'd left her, buried up to her neck. It was four in the afternoon. A cool breeze stirred the sand, and you could walk now without stepping on the sides of your feet. I stopped a couple feet away, wondering if I should let her sleep, but then Shorty dawdled over and began to sniff her face. My mother started, then yelled at me to take off her sunglasses.

'Why?'

'I'm afraid to move.'

I knelt down and did as my mother asked. There was something caught in her eyelashes: a perfect jewel, glittering in the sun.

'We can't afford to lose it,' she said.

She shut her eye very slowly, like an owl, and I reached down with two fingers and plucked the crumpled contact lens from her lashes. Tweezed between my fingers, it really did look like a diamond. I cupped my other hand around it, trying to protect it from the breeze. My mother took some time getting to her feet, but I didn't complain. Anyway, this was our life now.

She found a Kleenex and we wrapped the lens up like a tooth and stuck it in her purse. My mother stared at me with one eye screwed shut, covered head to toe in sand. She looked less drunk, as if popping out of the ground had refreshed her somehow. Ranger bared his teeth and growled.

'He doesn't recognize you.'

'Good,' she said strangely. She brushed the sand from her arms and legs as best she could, and squinted one-eyed down the beach.

'He's gone,' I said.

She nodded. The breeze had sharpened to a wind, and the waves were getting blown out, dark patches flickering across the water and misting the tops of them. You could smell the salt in the air, stronger than before. My mother bent down and rubbed her legs, which were covered in goosebumps.

'It's getting chilly out here,' she said. She closed both eyes for a moment, as if she were feeling woozy. 'Can I have some of your coffee?'

I went over and grabbed the cup of cold coffee from the sand and handed it to her. She took a sip and grimaced.

'You really like this stuff?'

'No,' I said. I handed her the sunglasses.

'You might like it in a couple years.'

I tried to imagine what I'd look like in a couple years, and where we'd be living, and how the hell my mother would manage to support us. I tried to imagine this, but I couldn't. I looked toward the water and could see the curve of the earth, way out where the ocean faded into a strip of white, a lone barge out there shimmering on the horizon, still and dainty as a toy, and for a moment the wind at my shirt seemed to blow right through me.

My mother poured the dregs of her Slurpee out, and the dogs sniffed over to the damp spot in the sand, bumping noses. My mom watched them for a while, pink already with sunburn, her glasses reflecting a smaller version of the world, as if the beach and crashing waves and vacant lifeguard stand were as far away as that boat on the horizon, and I could see why Ranger had barked at her. She looked unrecognizable to me, too.

'Why did you say that to that beachcomber?' I asked.

'Which part?'

'That you can walk on your hands?'

My mother looked at me humbly. Then she walked toward the water where the sand was firmer. She got down on all fours and jumped her legs up so she was standing on her hands, bent like a scorpion's tail, the skirt of her dress hanging down around her. You could see her underwear – plain as a man's briefs – but at that moment I was too astounded to care. She walked that way for a few steps, teetering along on her hands and scaring up a puff of kelp flies. A wave foamed between her fingers, dampening the ends of her hair, but she didn't stop. I had the sense that this was the only time I'd ever see her do this. After today, we wouldn't have the chance. But she could still do it now; she could surprise me with a useless talent. The sun flashed behind her, flickering between her legs, and someone watching from down the beach might even have mistaken us for two kids. She teetered on like that, on the verge of falling, while Shorty and Ranger barked and splashed around her, wagging their stubby little tails, no idea what was next. ■

New Tarzon Guided Bomb Hits Bull's-Eye!

Bomb With A Brain Aka "The Tarzon" Guides Itself To Targets

A secret new wonder bomb, the result of exhaustive testing and experimentation, is dropped from a B-29 over a secret proving ground somewhere in the United States. At first the bomb, called Tarzon, merely seems to fall, then as if guided by an invisible hand, moves off to the right to follow the line below. At the end of the line is the target, which the bomb seeks out with an eerie, almost human understanding. Watch this performance carefully, for you are witnessing a new concept of modern warfare. Now the bomb holds fast to the line. The

America's secret new wonder bomb, the Tarzon, is dropped over a hush-hush testing ground somewhere in the United States. At first glance, it appears to be rather like a V-1 rocket the Germans used to fire at southern England. But now it moves to the right to follow the road below as if guided by some invisible hand. At the end of the long road is the target, which the bomb seeks out with an uncanny, almost human understanding. The target's not far off now, and the bomb's still holding fast to its path. The circular target area is below, and

Air Force refuses to give details of the Tarzon's operation and range, but it hits the bull's-eye as the bombardier intended. That was a practice run. Now, in actual combat in Korea, the guided bomb seeks out the underwater structure of a dam vital to the Reds. Again a perfect bull's-eye. Is the Tarzon in mass production? Is it used regularly in Korea? The Air Force doesn't say. Still more sensational films show the Tarzon seeking out a bridge. Loaded with an atomic warhead, the Tarzon could be the world's most terrifying weapon.

down goes the Tarzon. That was a practice run, but in action in Korea the bomb is released to seek out the underwater structure of a dam vital to the Reds. Another bull's-eye. The American Air Force refuses to give any details of the Tarzon's range and operation. Now the bomb attacks an enemy-held bridge. Loaded with an atomic warhead the Tarzon might well be one of the world's most powerful weapons.

NOTES ON THE POEMS: 'New Tarzon Guided Bomb Hits Bull's-Eye!' (American voice-over) and 'Bomb With A Brain Aka "The Tarzon" Guides Itself To Targets' (British voice-over): narration borrowed from British Pathé 1952 newsreel.

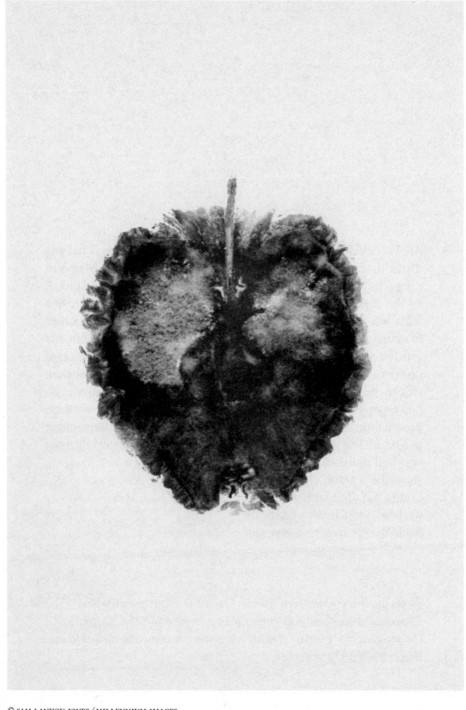

THE WAY OF THE APPLE WORM

Herta Müller

TRANSLATED FROM THE GERMAN BY PHILIP BOEHM

The ant is carrying a dead fly three times its size. The ant can't see the way ahead, it flips the fly around and crawls back. Adina doesn't want to block the ant's path so she pulls in her elbow. A clump of tar next to her knee glistens as it seethes in the sun. Adina dabs at the tar with her finger, raising a thin thread that stiffens in the air before it snaps.

The ant has the head of a pin, the sun can't find any place to burn. The sun stings. The ant loses its way. It crawls but is not alive, the human eye does not consider it an animal. The spike-heads of the grasses on the outskirts of town crawl the same way. The fly is alive because it's three times the size of the ant and because it's being carried, the human eye does consider the fly an animal.

Clara is blinded by the blazing pumpkin of the sun and doesn't see the fly. She sits with her legs apart and rests her hands between her knees. Pubic hair shows where her swimsuit cuts into her thighs. Below her pubic hair is a pair of scissors, a spool of white thread, sunglasses and a thimble. Clara is sewing a summer blouse for herself. The needle dives, the thread advances, the needle pricks her finger and Clara licks the blood and spits out a shorthand curse involving ice and thread: your mother on the ice. A curse implying unspeakable things done to the mother of the needle. When Clara curses, everything has a mother.

The mother of the needle is the place that bleeds. The mother of the needle is the oldest needle in the world, the one that gave birth to all needles. The mother of the needle watches out for all her children, she is always looking for a finger to stab on every sewing hand in the world. The world contained in the curse is tiny, tucked under a cluster of needles and a clot of blood. And the mother of all thread is there too, lurking inside the curse, a massive tangle looming over the world.

All this heat and you're going on about ice, says Adina, as Clara's jawbones grind away while her tongue beats inside her mouth. Whenever she curses, Clara's face wrinkles up, because every word is a well-aimed bullet fired from her lips and every word hits its mark. As well as the mother of its mark.

Clara lies down on the blanket next to Adina. Adina is naked, Clara is wearing her swimsuit bottoms and nothing else.

Curses are cold. They have no need of dahlias or bread or apples or summer. Curses are not for smelling and not for eating. Only for churning up and laying down flat, for an instant of rage and a long time keeping still. Curses lower the throbbing of the temples into the wrist and hoist the dull heartbeat into the ear. Curses swell and choke on themselves.

Once a curse is lifted, it never existed.

The blanket is spread out on the roof of the apartment block, which is surrounded by poplars. The poplars rise higher than all the city roofs and are draped with green, they don't show individual leaves, only a wash of foliage. They don't swish, they whoosh. The foliage rises straight up on the poplars just like the branches, the wood cannot be seen. And where nothing else can reach, the poplars carve the hot air. The poplars are green knives.

When Adina stares at the poplars too long, they dig their knives inside her throat and twist them from side to side. Then her throat gets dizzy. And her forehead senses that no afternoon is capable of holding even a single poplar for the time the light takes to sink behind the factory into the evening. The evening ought to hurry, the night might succeed in holding the poplars, because then they can't be seen.

The day is shattered by the beating of rugs between apartment blocks, the blows echo up to the roof and collapse one onto the other, the way Clara's words do when she curses.

The beating of rugs cannot hoist the dull heartbeat into the ear.

Clara is tired after her curse, and the sky is so empty she closes her eyes, which are blinded by the light, while Adina opens her eyes wide and gazes far too long into the emptiness. From high overhead, beyond the reach even of the green knives, a taut thread of hot air stretches straight down to her eyes. And from this thread hangs the weight of the city.

That morning at school a child said to Adina, the sky looks so different today. A boy who's always very still when he's with the others. His eyes are set far apart, which makes his temples look narrow. My mother woke me up at four o'clock this morning, he said, and gave me the key because she had to go to the train station. I walked out to the gate with her. When we were going through the courtyard the sky was so close I could feel it on my shoulder. I could have leaned back against it, but I didn't want to scare my mother. When I went back by myself I could see right through all the stones. So I hurried as fast as I could. The door to our building looked different, the wood was empty. I could have slept another three hours, the child said, but I never fell back asleep. And even though I hadn't slept I still woke up scared. Only maybe I really did sleep, because my eyes felt all pinched up. I had this dream that I was lying in the sun next to the water and I had this blister on my stomach. I pulled the skin off the blister but it didn't hurt. Because under my skin was stone. Then the wind blew and lifted the water into the air, but it wasn't water at all, just a wrinkled cloth. And there weren't any stones underneath either, only flesh.

The boy laughed into that last sentence, and into the silence that followed. His teeth were like gravel, the blackened half-teeth and the smooth white ones. The age in his face couldn't stand his childish voice. The boy's face smelled like stale fruit.

It was the smell of old women who put on so much powder it starts to wilt just like their skin. Women whose hands quiver in front of the mirror, who smudge lipstick on their teeth and then a little while later inspect their fingers against the mirror. Whose nails are buffed and ringed with white.

When the boy stood in the schoolyard together with the other children, the blotch on his cheek was the clamp of loneliness. And the spot grew, because slanting light was falling over the poplars.

Clara has dozed off in the sun, her sleep carries her far away and leaves Adina alone. The beating of rugs shatters the summer into shells of green. And the whoosh of the poplars contains the green shells of all the summers left behind. All the years when you're still a child and growing and nevertheless sense that each single day goes tumbling off some cliff whenever evening comes. Days of childhood, with square-cut hair and dried mud in the outskirts of town, dust behind the streetcar, and on the sidewalk the footsteps of tall, emaciated men earning money to buy bread.

The outskirts were attached to the town with wires and pipes and a bridge that had no river. The outskirts were open at both ends, just like the walls, the roads and the lines of trees. The city streetcars went whooshing into the town at one of the ends, where the factories blew smoke into the sky above the bridge that had no river. At times the whooshing and the smoke were all the same thing. At the other end, farmland gnawed away at the outskirts, and the fields of leafy beets stretched far into the countryside. Further away still was a village, the white walls gleaming in the distance looked no bigger than a hand. Suspended between the village and the bridge that had no river were sheep. The sheep didn't eat the beet leaves, only the grass that grew along the way, before the summer was out they had devoured the entire lane. Then they gathered at the edge of town and licked the walls of the factory.

The factory was large, with buildings on both sides of the bridge without water. From behind the walls came the screaming of cows and pigs. At night their horns and hooves were burned, the acrid stench wafted into the outskirts. The factory was a slaughterhouse.

In the morning, while it was still dark, roosters crowed. They walked through the gray inner courtyards the same way the emaciated men walked on the street. And they had the same look.

The men rode the streetcar to the last stop and then crossed the bridge. On the bridge the sky hung low, and when it was red, the men had red cockscombs in their hair. The local barber told Adina's father that there was nothing more beautiful than a cockscomb for the heroes of labor.

Adina had asked the barber about the red combs because he knew every scalp and every whorl. He said whorls are for hair what wings are for roosters. So even though no one could say exactly when, Adina knew that each of the emaciated men would at some point go flying over the bridge.

Because sometimes the roosters did go flying over the fences. Before taking off they would drink water out of empty food cans in the courtyards. At night the roosters slept in shoeboxes. When the trees turned cold at night, cats crawled into the boxes as well.

It was exactly seventy steps from the last stop to the bridge that had no river – Adina had counted them. The last stop on one side of the street was the first on the other. At the last stop the men climbed out slowly, and at the first the women climbed in quickly. Early in the morning they ran to catch the streetcar with matted hair and flying purses and sweat stains under their arms. The stains were often dried out and rimmed with white. Their nail polish was eaten away by machine oil and rust. And even as they rushed to catch the streetcar their faces already carried the weariness from the wire factory.

At the sound of the first streetcars Adina woke up. She felt cold in her summer dress. The dress had a pattern of trees, but the tops were upside down. The seamstress had stitched the material the wrong way.

The seamstress lived in two small rooms, the floor was full of angles and the walls had bellied out from the damp. The windows opened onto the courtyard. One window had a sign propped up that said COOPERATIVE OF PROGRESS.

The seamstress called the rooms the WORKSHOP. Every surface – table, bed, chairs, chest and even the floor – was covered with snippets and scraps. And each piece of fabric had a piece of paper with a name. A wooden crate behind the bed held a sack full of scraps. On the crate was a label NO LONGER OF USE.

The seamstress kept her clients' measurements in a small notebook. Anyone who'd been coming for years was considered a longtimer. Whoever came rarely, by chance, or only once was a short-termer. If a longtimer brought some material, the seamstress didn't need to take more measurements, except for one woman who went into the slaughterhouse every day and was as emaciated as the men – for her the seamstress had to take new measurements every time. She held the tape in her mouth and said, really, you'd be better off going to the vet and having him outfit you with a dress instead of me. Every summer you get thinner and thinner. Pretty soon my notebook will get filled up with just your bones.

Several times a year the woman brought the seamstress a new notebook. On the cover it said BRIGADE NOTEBOOK and above the columns on each page it said LIVE WEIGHT and SLAUGHTER WEIGHT.

Adina was never allowed to go barefoot in the workshop, the scraps and snippets littering the floor were full of pins. Only the seamstress knew how to move without getting pricked. Once a week she crawled through the rooms with a magnet and all the pins and needles jumped into her hand.

When Adina tried on the dress, her mother said to the seamstress, can't you see that the trees are growing the wrong way, you turned the fabric upside down. The seamstress could still have turned it right side up, the fabric was only basted with white thread. But with two pins in her mouth she said, what's important is front and back, and that the zipper's on the left. Besides, when I look from here, the bottom is the top. She lowered her face to the floor. That's how the chickens see it, she said. And the dwarves, said Adina. Her mother looked out the window at the courtyard.

On the side of the courtyard that faced the street was a display window with crosses, stovepipes and watering cans made of tin. They were propped up with old newspapers, and in front of the display was an embroidered blanket with a tin sign on top that said COOPERATIVE OF PROGRESS.

The crosses, stovepipes and watering cans shuddered whenever the streetcar passed by. But they didn't tip over.

Behind the display window was a table with scissors, pliers and screws, behind the table sat a man. He was a tinsmith. He wore a leather apron. His wedding ring hung on a string around his neck, because both hands were missing the ring finger.

Some people said that his first wife had been dead a long time, and that he never found a second because he kept his wedding ring around his neck. The barber claimed that the tinsmith had never had a wife at all, that he'd used the same ring four times to get engaged but never married. If there were enough crosses, stovepipes and watering cans to fill the display window, he could turn to repairing old pots and pans.

When the streetcar passed, the faces in the tram hovered in the display window between the stovepipes and crosses. On the watering cans the faces were wavy from the movement and from the sheen of the tin. Once the streetcar moved on, the only thing left on the watering cans was the gleam of trampled snow.

For several summers Adina wore her dress with the falling trees. Every summer Adina grew, and the dress got shorter. And every summer the trees hung upside down and they felt as heavy as ever. Underneath the rising trees that lined the sidewalk, the girl from the outskirts of town had a shy face. The shade never covered it entirely. Her shaded cheek stayed cool, and Adina had the feeling she could zip it open or shut, like her dress. Her cheek in the sunlight turned hot and soft.

After a summer rain that failed to cool off the paving stones, black chains of ants crawled inside the cracks in the courtyard. Adina took a tube from a circular knitting needle and poured sugar water into the transparent plastic and set the tube in one of the cracks. The ants crawled inside and lined up: head, abdomen, head, abdomen. Adina lit a match, sealed the ends of the tube and hung it around her neck. Stepping to the mirror she saw that the necklace was alive, even though the ants were dead, stuck to the sugar, each in the place where it had suffocated.

Only when the ants were in the tube did the human eye consider them animals.

Adina went to the barber every week, because her hair grew quickly and she wasn't allowed to let it cover her ears. On the way she passed the display window with the crosses, stovepipes and watering cans. The tinsmith waved and she went inside. He handed her a cone rolled from newspaper. The cone had cherries in May, apricots as early as June, and grapes just a little later, even though no ripe ones could be found in any of the gardens. At the time Adina was convinced that the newspaper caused the change of fruit.

When he handed her the cone the tinsmith said, eat the fruit now or else it'll go bad. And she started to eat very quickly, fearing it might go bad even while he was talking. Then the tinsmith said, eat slowly so you can savor every bite for a long time.

She chewed and swallowed and watched as the flame flickered from the soldering iron, covering and filling the pits in the bottom of the pot. The filled holes gleamed like the stovepipes, watering cans and crosses in the window. When fire stops chewing your pot, death will bite you in the ass, said the tinsmith.

One afternoon Adina went to get her hair cut wearing her necklace of ants. She sat in front of the big mirror and let her legs dangle off the chair. The barber combed down her hair and when he reached her neck he stopped, shielded his eyes with the comb, and said, that's it, either the ants go this minute or else you do.

A man was sleeping in the corner. The barber's cat was sprawled across his thighs, also sleeping. The man was emaciated and had a cockscomb every morning when he crossed the bridge on his way to the slaughterhouse. He woke with a start and flung the cat out the door. I've got enough dead animals in the slaughterhouse, he shouted, then spat on the floor.

The floor was matted with hair clippings from emaciated men who all knew one another. The hair was brittle, dark gray, light gray and white and made the floor seem like a giant scalp. Cockroaches crawled among the strands. The hair moved up and down. The hair was alive because it was being carried by the cockroaches. But it was not alive on the heads of the men.

The barber dropped his scissors into the open drawer, I can't cut your hair like this, he said, I can feel the ants crawling inside my clothes. He jerked his shirt out of his pants and scratched himself. His fingers left red marks on his stomach. Mother of ants, he cursed. Mother of corpses, said the man from the slaughterhouse. Suddenly the mirror moved and Adina saw herself cut off by the drawer, her feet looked like they were hanging from a roof. She ran out the door and past the cat, who gazed after her with more than its own two eyes.

A week later the barber gave Adina some sweets. The candy had hair sticking to it that scratched her tongue. Adina tried to spit out the hair, but the barber told her it was good for cleaning the throat.

The candy scratched inside her mouth and Adina asked when the man who had flung the cat outside was going to die. The barber crammed a handful of candy into his mouth and said, when a man's had enough hair cut to fill a stamped-down sack, and the sack weighs the same as the man, the man dies. I put all the men's hair into a sack and stamp it down and wait until it's full, said the barber. I don't weigh the hair on the scale, I weigh it with my eyes. I know how much hair I've cut off every person over the years. My eyes can feel the weight. And I'm never mistaken. He blew on the back of Adina's neck.

The client who threw out the cat will come here seven or eight more times, he said. That's why I didn't say anything, even though the cat hasn't eaten a thing since. I don't want to send a longtime client into the unknown with some other barber for his last haircuts. A wrinkle curled up from his mouth and sliced into his cheek.

Clara sits up on the blanket to put on her summer blouse. The thimble on her forefinger burns in the sun. Her legs are bony, in one motion she pulls them close to her chest and rocks forward as she puts on the blouse. It's the movement of a bony bird who doesn't need to do anything except gaze into the summer and be beautiful. The nearby poplar knife watches. The stubble growing back inside her shaved armpits has already turned into the chin of the man she's talking about. A man with style, she says, is someone I've never met. But I wish.

Clara laughs and straightens out her legs. Her wish is stoked by the sun and dizzied by the roof. Her head knows nothing of the green knives of the poplars, the edge of the roof, the clouds, the city. And that this roof in the sun is full of ants carrying dead flies. And that this roof in the sun is nothing more than a cliff in the sky.

The summer dress with the falling trees and the zipper made Adina forever wary of clothes. She often went to the seamstress's workshop, where she would measure the lives of the women by the weight of the fabric scraps. She would sit and watch, determined to size up each client. She knew which woman's scraps would soon fill a stamped-down sack that weighed as much as the woman. And that after four more dresses, the woman from the slaughterhouse would die.

Clara takes a small, red-flecked summer apple out of her bag and holds it under Adina's chin. The thimble glows, its sharp edge barely missing the apple skin. A small apple with a long, woody stem that takes up too much of what should have been flesh. Adina takes a deep bite. Spit it out, says Clara, there's a worm. The fruit is burrowed with a brown, crumbly thread. Adina swallows what she's bitten off, worm and all. It's just an apple worm, she says, it grows inside the apple, it's made of apple flesh. It doesn't grow inside the apple, says Clara, it crawls inside, eats its way through and then crawls back out. That is its way.

Adina eats, the bite crunches in her ear, what's it supposed to do outside, she says, it's nothing but apple, it's white and eats white flesh and shits a brown path, once it eats its way through the apple it dies. That is its way.

Clara's eyes are small and without any makeup. The sky is empty and the poplar knives stand upright and green. Clara says nothing, she lies down on the blanket, her pupils roll down straight toward her mouth and her eyes close.

A cloud hangs over the apartment block, white and churning. Old folk who die in summer float for a while above the city, lingering between bed and grave.

Clara and the summer old folk are lying in the same sleep. Adina feels the way of the apple worm in her stomach. It runs through her pubic hair down the inside of her thighs and into the hollows of her knees. ∎

© MALCOLM CROUCHMAN
Thornham Marshes, 2009

COVENTRY

Rachel Cusk

E very so often, for offences actual or hypothetical, my mother
and father stop speaking to me. There's a funny phrase for this
phenomenon in England: it's called being sent to Coventry. I don't
know what the origins of the expression are, though I suppose I could
easily find out. Coventry suffered badly in the war: it once had a
beautiful cathedral that in 1940 was bombed into non-existence.
Now it's an ordinary town in the Midlands, and if it hasn't made
sense of its losses, it has at least survived them.

Sometimes it takes me a while to notice that my parents have sent
me to Coventry. It's not unlike when a central-heating boiler breaks
down: there's no explosion, no dramatic sight or sound, merely a
growing feeling of discomfort that comes from the gradual drop in
temperature, and that one might be surprisingly slow – depending on
one's instinct for habituation – to attribute to an actual cause. Like
coldness the silence advances, making itself known not by presence
but by absence, by disturbances of expectation so small that they
are registered only half-consciously and instead mount up, so that
one only becomes truly aware of it once its progress is complete.
It takes patience to send someone to Coventry: it's not a game for
those who require instant satisfaction. If you don't live with your
victim or see them every day, it might be a while before they even

notice they've been sent there. All the same, there's no mistaking this for anything less deliberate than punishment. It is the attempt to recover power through withdrawal, rather as the powerless child indignantly imagines his own death as a punishment to others. *Then they'll be sorry!* It's a gamble, with oneself as the stakes. My mother and father seem to believe they are inflicting a terrible loss on me by disappearing from my life. They appear to be wielding power, but I've come to understand that their silence is the opposite of power. It is in fact failure, their failure to control the story, their failure to control me. It is a failure so profound that all they have left to throw at it is the value of their own selves, like desperate people taking the last of their possessions to the pawn shop.

But perhaps it isn't like that at all. I remember girls being sent to Coventry at school, a cold and calculated process of exclusion in which the whole cohort would participate. It was a test of an individual's capacity for survival, of her psychological strength: if other people pretend you're not there, how long can you go on believing you exist? This was elemental bullying, the deliberate removal of the relational basis of human reality. The group would watch their victim with interest, as she wandered wordless and unacknowledged through the days. By sending someone to Coventry you are in a sense positing the idea of their annihilation, asking how the world would look without them in it. Perversely, over time, your victim might cultivate exaggerated notions of their own importance, for this troubling fact of their existence seems to have an unusual significance. Sometimes, at school, a person could ultimately gain power by surviving a visit to Coventry. It is a place of fragments and ruins: I've seen a photograph of the cathedral the day after its bombardment, a few smoking walls standing in an ocean of glittering shards, as if the sky itself had fallen to the earth and shattered. What the image states is that everything, no matter how precious and beautiful, no matter how painstakingly built and preserved, no matter how apparently timeless and resilient, can be broken. That was the world my parents were born into, a world where sacred monuments could disappear between bedtime and breakfast, a world at war: it is perhaps no surprise then, that war remains their model. War is a narrative: it might almost be said to embody the narrative principle itself. It is the attempt to create a story of life, to create agreement. In war, there is no point of view; war is the end of point of view, where violence is welcomed as the final means of arriving at a common version of events. It never occurred to me that instead of sending me to Coventry, my parents might simply have picked up the phone and set things to right in person. That isn't how stories work. For a start, it's far too economical. The generation of a narrative entails a lot of waste. In the state of war, humans are utterly abandoned to waste in the pursuit of victory. Yet in all the many times I've been sent to Coventry, this question of waste is one I've never really addressed. Sometimes I've been surprised to find myself there again; at other times merely resigned. I've been dismayed, upset, angry, ashamed. I've felt defiant, self-critical, abject; I've gone over and over events, trying to see where I made the mistake, trying to find the crime that might be equal to the punishment, trying to see my own unacceptability like trying to see a ghost in the cold light of day. The thing about Coventry is that it has no words: nothing is explained to you there, nothing made clear. It is entirely representational. And what I've never felt about it, I realise, is indifference.

I have a woman friend whose children are starting to leave home. The eldest has gone to university; now the second is filling out application forms, as the others will do in their turn. It's a big family, steady as an ocean liner. There's been no divorce, no disaster; any minor difficulties or discrepancies that have arisen over the years have been carefully toned down and blended back into the picture. Sometimes, talking to my friend, it has occurred to me that even if there had been a disaster, I wouldn't necessarily know about it; that in fact her very definition of a disaster might be 'an event impossible to conceal'. This quality in her, this ability to maintain the surface, has always struck me as a form of courage; indeed, I have vaguely considered her to be the adult in our relationship, though we are more or less the same age. But lately things have changed – or perhaps it would be more accurate to say, since change always implies at least some possibility of renewal, that they have deteriorated. Like an actor coming out of character onstage, there is evidence of slippage, of a loss of frequency in my friend's persona, as though she is losing belief in what she is doing. She has started to talk too much, or not at all, or in non sequiturs; she produces observations out of unfathomable silences, as though laboriously drawing up from the bottom of a well things that have lain there undisturbed for years. It is clear her mind is moving on a different track, away into uncharted distances. One afternoon, at her house, she talks about a feeling she's been having lately – that she'd like to see, piled up in a great mountain, all the things that have been bought and thrown away over the course of their family life. All the toys and the tricycles, the Barbie dolls, the babygros, the cribs and the chemistry sets, the outgrown shoes and clothes, the abandoned violins and sports equipment, the bright crumpled paper plates from birthday parties, the Christmas trinkets, the souvenirs, the tat from countless gift shops acquired on countless days out, the faddish electronics – everything whose purchase had at the time seemed to offer a solution to something, and whose disposal later on a better solution still: she would like to see it all again, not for the sake of nostalgia but to get the measure of it as objective fact. My friend is admittedly something of a materialist: from the beginning, her enactment of family life was played out amid a substantive and ever-changing set of props. She governed this world of possession with one cardinal rule: every time something new was acquired, something old had to be disposed of. Like a spring of fresh water running through a pond, this mechanism had seemed to avert the danger of stagnation. But now a different possibility appeared to be occurring to her: that it had all been, in the end, a waste.

Stories only work – or so we're always being told – through the suspension of our disbelief. It's never been altogether clear to me whether our disbelief is something that ought to be suspended for us, or whether we're expected deliberately to suspend it ourselves.

There's an idea that a successful narrative is one that gives you no choice in the matter; but mostly I imagine it's a question of both sides conspiring to keep the suspension aloft. Being sent to Coventry is perhaps an example of such a conspiracy: it would be hard to send someone to Coventry who refused to believe they were there, just as it's hard to fight a pacifist. Much of my being in Coventry, I now realise, lay in my willingness to recognise and accept the state of being outcast. I suspended my disbelief and, having done so I jeopardised, in some sense, my relationship with reality. Like gravity, truth can only be resisted for so long: it waits, greyly, for the fantasy to wear off. My friend's concern with the material evidence of her family life likewise seems to me to be a concern about truth. It is as though each of the many objects that passed through her home over the years represents a lost fragment of reality. She believed in all of it, at the time, believed passionately in the Barbie doll and the violin and the Nintendo that everyone had to have one year – and once the belief had worn off, these things were thrown away. But what, had she not believed in them, might she have seen instead? In the suspension of her disbelief, what did she miss? It is almost as if she feels that the true story of her family has eluded her; and that the mountain of discarded possessions, like a mountain of unopened husks, would represent the size and scale of the mystery.

M y husband has observed that two thirds of our conversation is spent discussing our children. He is not the father of my children, and I am not the mother of his. We're like the chief executives of a large corporation: we're in the business of successful management rather than sentimentality. He is careful not to posit this claim as a Bad Thing – it's just a fact, which may or may not be avoidable. Or rather, it's a choice. In choosing to spend two thirds of our time talking about our children, we are perhaps choosing to re-enter the narrative paradigm. We are starting to tell the story again. We are suspending our disbelief.

He doesn't imply that it's my choice more than his, though history makes that the supposition. In marriage, the woman compensates for her lack of external power by commandeering the story. Isn't that right? She fills the silence, the mystery of her own acts and aims with a structured account of life whose relationship to the truth might sometimes be described as voluntary. I am familiar with that account: I spent my childhood listening to it. And what I noticed was how, over the years, its repetitions and elisions and exaggerations ceased to exasperate its listeners so much as silence them. After a while, people stopped bothering to try to put the record straight: on the contrary, they became, in a curious way, dependent on the teller of this tale, in which they featured as central characters. The sheer energy and wilful, self-constructing logic of narrative, which at first made one cringe and protest every time the truth was dented, came over time to seem preferable to elusive, chaotic reality.

My husband and I have both come from other marriages: at a certain point our disbelief came crashing down on our heads like the roof of Coventry Cathedral. We live on the coast now, in a village holidaymakers of a certain age like to visit. In the local pub we watch tourist couples sitting in silence over enormous platters of fish and chips. It is unwise, I have learned, to put one's faith in how things look, but it's not often that silence presents itself as a visual event. And other people, it seems, notice the silent couples too. Like the seal colony out on the sound, it turns out they're a sort of local feature. The waiters in the pub treat them with especial tenderness; children gaze at them with what might be wonderment or concern. Our friends discuss them, the men with nervous jocularity, the women with a remote and finely judged pity. Everyone agrees that it is sad. I notice that they are often very well turned out, the woman carefully made up, the man pressed and groomed. They sit erect among the untidy holidaying families with their shoals of tousle-haired children, their dogs, their footballs and frisbees and bicycles, their aura of action and noise as they pass through life like a company of soldiers going over the top. The families are on display – it's part of how they function. Families tend to be conscious of being looked at:

they perform themselves as though in expectation of a response, a judgement. I suppose they are exposing what they have created, as an artist feels compelled to do. The exposure ought, in a sense, to correct the subjectivity of parenthood, though it doesn't always seem to work like that. There are families whose children run through the pub shouting and laughing and knocking over chairs. There are families where the children sit miserably at the table with downcast eyes while their parents relentlessly chastise them. Jacob, you're annoying the lady, says one mother, mildly and with unmistakable pride, while her son fires his water pistol at another child across my table. Your needs aren't a priority right now, a father is saying at a table on the other side. He is addressing a pallid girl of six or seven, with square-framed glasses and hair in tight, flaxen plaits tied with ribbons. You always get your own way, he adds, raising his glass slowly to his lips.

The silent couples display themselves too, but theirs is an exposure far more mysterious. They sit like monuments, like commemorations of some opaque history: in their silence and their stillness time seems almost to come to a halt. They are like effigies of the dead standing among the living, mute and motionless amid the helter-skelter families and the noise and bustle of the pub. They eat slowly, carefully; they don't, as a rule, look at one another. It is as if, each in themselves, they are alone. I wonder why they have come to this public place to enact their silence. They seem to represent failure: have they come to warn us, like ghosts from purgatory might enjoin us to mend our ways lest we too get caught on the treadmill of our sins? Or have they come just to warm themselves for a few hours with the conversation of others? It could be supposed that they are unhappy, but I wonder whether this is true. Perhaps what they represent is not the failure of narrative but its surpassing, not silence but peace. They are all talked out: this is a notion other people find unsettling. It can be assumed that many of the silent couples have children, now grown up and gone away. What other people don't like, I suppose, is the idea that on the other side of all that effort, all those years of joy and toil and creation, all that suspension of disbelief, there is nothing – or nothing palpable

– to look forward to; that one might wake from family life as from a bacchanal into the cold light of day. I wonder whether the silent couples once spent two thirds – or more – of their time talking about their children. I wonder whether their silence represents the problem of reconnecting to reality once the story has ended.

In the day I often walk on the salt marsh, along the coastal path. The marsh is flat and low-lying: from a distance it is merely a strip of grey or brown, banded by the blue line of the sea. It is reached by descending through a copse of trees whose trunks have been sculpted and bleached over time into strange, pale forms by the coastal weather. They glimmer in the copse's half-light like headless bodies held in curious, balletic poses; they are both sensual and unearthly, like a race of nymphs with the glade as their home. The path winds amongst them and out the other side, down to the place where the marsh meets the land. There is always something startling about arriving out of the trees on to the marsh. No matter how much you try to retain its image, the physical sensation of arrival there presents itself anew. It is a feeling of clarity and expansion, as though a word you'd been trying and trying to remember had suddenly come back to you. The marsh has many moods, so it's curious that it delivers these sensations so unfailingly. It is an involuted landscape whose creeks form intestinal patterns amid the springy furze. Twice a day the tide fills these channels silently with water beneath the huge dome of the sky: narrow and deep, they shine like a maze of open cuts. If you try to walk out across it to the sea, you quickly find yourself unable to progress. In Venice, the uninitiated attempt to travel by following their sense of direction and unfailingly get lost, obstructed by the blank walls of culs-de-sac or cut off by a canal with their destination tantalisingly close across the water. Venice obfuscates the notions of progress and self-will, and the marsh does the same. There are paths, but so narrow and faint as to be recognisable only to those who know they are there. The one nearest our house is called the Baitdiggers, the product of years – perhaps centuries – of accumulated knowledge, the knowledge of men who had to trudge across the marsh in all

weathers to dig in the distant sands for worms, and who finally
identified the merest thread of land that travelled through the sunken
archipelago in a more or less straight line from one point to the other.
Knowledge is so slender and hard-won, and ignorance so vast and
dangerous. Usually I keep to the coast path, a well-travelled route
that skirts these tensions. Often I meet the holidaying families there,
in their diurnal guises. From a distance, across the flat landscape, they
are tiny figures moving untidily but with an overarching logic, like
scraps being blown along by a directional wind. They advance slowly
but inexorably, scattering and regrouping, occasionally pausing as
though snagged on some obstacle. As they get closer the pattern
becomes more readable and distinct; the figures acquire identity, the
story begins to shape itself. They become recognisable as mother,
father, children; their movements begin to form the integument of
narrative. The scattering and regrouping becomes a meaningful
drama of self and others, of human emotion. I watch this drama
as it approaches across the marsh, as though on a moving stage. I
notice that the adults are often separated: one will walk musingly
ahead or behind while the other herds the children along the path.
Occasionally they will change roles, like a changing of the guard. The
herding parent is released and the solitary muser will rejoin the family
reality. I often study the lone parent as they pass, noting the particular
quality of their self-absorption. They don't, as a rule, look like people
taking in their surroundings: theirs is the self-absorption of someone
driving a car through long distances, seeing the world but shut off
from it, both free and unfree.

Like any drama, this one involves a lot of talking. I listen to
the familiar lines, the cadences of call and response, the river
of commentary, the chastisements and encouragements, the
opportunities for humour and tension navigated badly or well. The
parental script and the script of childhood are more or less adhered
to; the performances vary. Excess, the writer Aharon Appelfeld said,
is the enemy of art: and it's true that from the outside the family
drama is imperilled as a form by the exaggeration of any of its

constituent parts, by too much love or too much anger, too much laxity or discipline, too much honesty or not enough. Sometimes, as I watch, the families cross one or other of these boundaries, and I am struck then by the difference between the people inside the drama and the people watching. Often the family actors aren't aware that they've made their audience wince. I remember once, herding my small children through Paris, an elegant elderly man approaching us along the pavement, clearly intending to speak. I remember wondering what he wanted; I remember thinking, vaguely, that he might be going to congratulate us. As he reached me, he raised a long, slender finger to his lips and made a sshing sound. Madame, he said, too much noise.

I am a woman of nearly forty-nine, nearly fifty. My children are teenagers; they spend some of their time with me and some with their father. The family script we once followed was abandoned long ago: the stage was struck; that play is no longer performed. I am conscious sometimes of the fact that no new script has come to replace it. There have been pilots, synopses, ideas thrown around; but fundamentally, the future is a blank. For my children that blank is perhaps subsumed into the greater question of what and how they will be in their lives; a patch of thin ice, as it were, at the brink of a larger and more solid expanse of untried whiteness. For me, the possibilities are less clear. Throughout my adult life, I have used the need to earn money as the central support of a sense of self-justification: as a woman, that always seemed at least preferable to the alternatives. The need still remains, of course, but increasingly I find it less of a spur. I struggle to suspend my disbelief, but in what? What is there left to disbelieve in?

One weekend, my parents come to stay. It is winter; the coast path is frozen into ruts of black mud and the darkness starts to fall at four o'clock. My husband and I make the house as welcoming as we can. We turn the heating up and put flowers in the rooms. My husband prepares an elaborate meal. When my parents arrive we give them glasses of champagne. But when they leave in their car on a hard and sparkling Sunday morning, I happen to glimpse their faces through the glittering windscreen just before they round the bend and see that their smiles have already vanished and their mouths are moving grimly in talk. I know then that it has happened again: I am going once more to Coventry.

A week of silence passes. My husband is surprised and a little affronted. He had expected a card, a call. He is not familiar with this world in which people accept your hospitality, eat your food and drink your wine and leave with every appearance of bonhomie, then cast you into the outer darkness. Finally he confesses: he believes it is his fault. Late on the last evening, he reminds me, when the dinner had been eaten and the wine drunk, he had brought up the subject of honesty. He had put his arm around me and asked my parents where they thought my honesty had come from. This, he is now convinced, has caused the rift, though he has no idea why: but he remembers feeling it, he says, at the time, a retraction, a jolt in his audience. He blurts it out like a child who has caused damage by playing with something he didn't understand; he wishes me to know it was unintentional.

While his comment may possibly have expedited my journey to Coventry, I know it wasn't the cause of my being sent there; yet his remarks have a strange effect on me. In the following weeks, as the silence grows and expands and solidifies, I find myself becoming, if not exactly fond, then increasingly accepting of it. All my life I have been terrified of Coventry, of its vastness and bleakness and loneliness, and of what it represents, which is ejection from the story. One is written out of the story of life like a minor character being written out of a soap opera. In the past I have usually been summoned back after a time, because the scriptwriters couldn't find a convincing enough reason for my disappearance: a family occasion or social event would arise whose appearance of normality my absence would threaten. And I have gone back eagerly, relievedly, like a dog being let back inside from the cold garden, for whom the possibilities of freedom are obscured by the need for acceptance and shelter. Once it has shown itself unwilling to be free, you can treat that dog how you like: it won't run away. Sometimes, in Coventry, I would ponder the idea of freedom. I believed occasionally that I was free. Freedom meant living in Coventry for ever and making the best of it; living amid the waste and shattered buildings, the desecrated past. It meant waking every day to the realisation that what once existed has now gone. It meant living in the knowledge of waste, of all one's endeavours having been pointless. It meant leaving the story unfinished, like a writer failing to complete the book that, whatever its qualities, has nonetheless been his life's work.

But this time, I start to feel safer in Coventry, safer in the silence. After all, Coventry is a place where the worst has already happened. Theoretically, there should be nothing there to fear. If some kind of accounting is called for, Coventry strikes me as a good place for that to occur. And I wonder whether, if I looked, I would find that other people had decided to come here too; had, as it were, sent themselves to Coventry, searching for the silence, for whatever truth might be found amid the smoking ruins of the story. My friend with her imaginary mountain of tat, for instance, or the silent couples in the pub. Who knows, I might even meet the Parisian gentleman here, and this time impress him with my reticence, my subtlety, my peace.

When I first met my husband I often didn't catch what he said. He spoke too quietly, or so it seemed to me; I'd ask him to repeat himself. He was often silent, and sometimes I found the silences unnerving. They caused me to feel panic, like a patch of thin ice: I feared it meant the story was faltering, breaking down; I feared it giving way beneath me. After a while they stopped making me nervous. It even gave me a sense of accomplishment to participate in them: like learning to ride a bicycle, silence was something that looked impossible from the outside but, once mastered, afforded a certain freedom. It demanded trust, trust in the dynamics. One can't teach someone to ride a bicycle by describing how it's done. A flight into the non-verbal is required. And so I tried it out, silence.

My husband, meanwhile, was trying out talking. After six months or so, he claimed that he had talked more in his time with me than in the whole of his previous life put together. I was struck by the quantity and richness of his vocabulary: it was as if he had opened a vault and showed me his collection of gold bars. I felt glad he'd decided to spend them on me. I have always lived among noisy people, laughers and bellowers, shouters and door-slammers; opinionated people, wits, people who tell good stories. In such company there were words that often got drowned out, shy words like empathy, mercy, gentleness, solicitude. That's not to say they weren't there – it's just that one didn't know for sure, and would forget to look for them in all the noise. My husband uses these words: I sit in Coventry, mulling them over. My parents send him an email, a birthday card, a card for his son; they seem to be inviting him to leave me there and rejoin the story. It seems they now feel they were perhaps a little careless, in how much they chose to waste; they'd like to recoup some of their losses. These approaches make him angry. He was adopted by his own parents as a baby: he does not take abandonment lightly. His father is dead now, but my husband tells me that in the days of their marriage his parents, on the rare occasions they went out for dinner, would often spend the evening in silence. They took pride in it; for them, he said, it signified that their intimacy was complete. When he and I look at the silent couples in the pub, then, we are perhaps seeing different things. My husband doesn't worship silence but he isn't afraid of it either. It is my parents, I begin to understand, who are afraid.

Summer comes: the marsh is dry, and warm underfoot. We take off our shoes to walk to the creek and swim. It is often windy on the marsh. The wind pours out of the flatness and the vastness, from the radial distances where the blue of the sky and the blue of the sea converge. The creek lies between the marsh and the beach, a desolate expanse of sand pockmarked with shells. It is a long, narrow declivity,

good for swimming: we remove our clothes, anchoring them against
the wind as best we can. I am shy of my body, even in this deserted,
primeval space. It is the body of a nearly 49-year-old, but it doesn't
feel that way. I have never felt myself to be ageing: on the contrary, I
have always had the strange sensation as time passes that I am getting
not older but younger. My body feels as though it has innocence as
its destination. This is not, of course, a physical reality – I view the
proof in the mirror with increasing puzzlement – but it is perhaps a
psychological one that conscripts the body into its workings. It is as
though I was born imprisoned in a block of stone from which it has
been both a necessity and an obligation to free myself. The feeling
of incarceration in what was pre-existing and inflexible works well
enough, I suppose, as a paradigm for the contemporary woman's
struggle towards personal liberty. She might feel it politically, socially,
linguistically, emotionally; I happen to have felt it physically. I am not
free yet, by any means. It is laborious and slow, chipping away at that
block. There would be a temptation to give up, were the feelings of
claustrophobia and confinement less intense.

The water in the creek is often surprisingly warm. After the first
shock, it is easy to stay in. It is perhaps thirty metres long and I swim
fast and methodically up and down. I don't like to talk or mess around
when I'm swimming; or it might be more accurate to say that I can't
imagine being able to mess around, can't imagine being free from
my own rules and ambitions, and more accurate still to say that I'm
frightened of what might happen if I were. Instead I set myself a
target and count the lengths. My husband dives in and swims for a
little while, slowly, without particular direction. Then he turns over
and lies on his back and floats, looking at the sky.

One day, over the summer, my parents send me an email. They
have some furniture they're getting rid of; they wonder whether
I want it. I reply, thanking them and declining. A few weeks later, my
mother calls and leaves a message. She would like to speak to me, she
says. She says she misses the children.

My daughters are an interesting hybrid of characteristics I have always believed to be irreconcilable. They are opinionated, but empathetic too; scarifyingly witty, but capable of gentleness and mercy. They don't waste these finer qualities on adults all that often – friendship is the ground on which they're currently building their lives. But they've been anxious about my presence in Coventry. They aren't familiar with war as the model for human relationships. They aren't used to things remaining fixed enough for the possibility of their destruction to be created. My parents' behaviour has caused them anger, but their forgiveness comes fast after it, like a dog chasing a rabbit: there's barely a beat between accusation and clemency. I'm vaguely aware that something is lost in the speed with which they accept wrongs being set back to rights. Is theirs to be a world without feuds, without lasting conflict, without Coventry, but also without memory? I tell them they are free to communicate with and see their grandparents as often as they please – they are old enough for that to be a reality – but that I myself don't wish to re-enter that arena. I don't want to leave Coventry. I've decided to stay.

They nod their heads, slightly mystified. They don't understand why I care so much. They don't understand why it matters. These are old things, old arguments, old people: it's so much ancient history. It is as though a moss-encrusted monument had suddenly tried to explain itself to them. I say to them, the thing about time is that it can transform the landscape without improving it. It can change everything except what needs to change.

They fidget, roll their eyes, check their phones.

That's really depressing, they say.

My husband and I have a plan, which is to visit certain artworks in the British Isles. I have spent a lot of time looking at art in other places but I have never seen, for instance, Stanley Spencer's paintings in the chapel at Burghclere in Hampshire. I have never visited Henry Moore's house in Much Hadham. I have never laid eyes on Simone Martini's *Christ Discovered at the Temple*, housed in the Walker Art Gallery in Liverpool. We'd like to do a tour that takes all these highlights in.

It's a good idea, though I don't know if it will ever become a reality. It's hard to find the time. There's always something, some new development, some incident or issue, some theme that needs attending to: the story still insists on telling itself, despite our best efforts to block our ears. If it does happen, one place we'll have to go is Coventry. In the aftermath of war, a generation of artists worked to create something afresh in the blasted city. A new cathedral was designed by Basil Spence to stand beside the ruins of the old: Benjamin Britten wrote his War Requiem to be premiered at its consecration. Graham Sutherland designed a vast tapestry for the interior; John Piper made the baptistry window, with its nearly two hundred panes; and John Hutton made his expressionist *Screen of Saints and Angels*. People were suspicious, apparently, of the cathedral's modernist design: when what you're used to is irretrievably gone, it's hard to believe in something new. But they suspended their disbelief. The new things came to be, became reality. What needed to change was changed, just as the old things were destroyed – not by time, but by force of human will. ■

CONTRIBUTORS

Azam Ahmed is a foreign correspondent for the *New York Times*. Formerly based in Kabul, he has written extensively on the Afghan war. He has also covered the advances of the Islamic State in Iraq.

Philip Boehm's translations from the German and Polish include works by Franz Kafka, Christoph Hein, Hanna Krall and Stefan Chwin. He is also a theatre director and playwright, and the author of *Mixtitlan, The Death of Atahualpa* and *Return of the Bedbug*. He lives in St Louis, where he is the artistic director of Upstream Theater.

Don Mee Choi is the author of *Hardly War, The Morning News Is Exciting*, and translator of contemporary Korean women poets. Her most recent works include the chapbook *Petite Manifesto* and the pamphlet *Freely Frayed, ㅋ=q, & Race=Nation*. She was born in Seoul and now lives in Seattle.

George Makana Clark was raised in Rhodesia. He is the author of the novel *The Raw Man* and the story collection *The Small Bees' Honey*. His work has appeared in *The Granta Book of the African Short Story, The O. Henry Prize Stories* and *Tin House*, among other publications. He teaches fiction writing and African literature at the University of Wisconsin-Milwaukee.

Rachel Cusk was one of *Granta*'s Best of Young British Novelists in 2003. She is the author of eight novels and three non-fiction works, including *Outline, Aftermath: On Marriage and Separation* and *The Country Life*.

Boris Dralyuk is a lecturer in Russian at the University of St Andrews. His most recent translation is *Red Cavalry* by Isaac Babel. He is co-editor of *The Penguin Book of Russian Poetry*.

Eliza Griswold's works include the poetry collection *Wideawake Field* and the non-fiction book *The Tenth Parallel*. Her poetry and reportage has appeared in the *New Yorker*, the *Atlantic*, the *New York Times Magazine* and *Harper's*. She is a senior fellow at the New America Foundation. 'Friday Afternoon with Boko Haram' is taken from a forthcoming poetry collection.

Peregrine Hodson is the author of *Under a Sickle Moon: A Journey Through Afghanistan* and *A Circle Round the Sun: A Foreigner in Japan, Inc.* 'Aftermath' is an excerpt from his forthcoming memoir, *A Hunter's Stone*.

A.M. Homes's most recent book is the novel *May We Be Forgiven*, winner of the 2013 Women's Prize for Fiction. She teaches at Princeton University and lives in New York city.

Eduardo Soteras Jalil is an Argentinian photographer. His projects include *En El Camino, Neutral Fire, Masafer: Life in the Interstice, All the Ices the Ice* and *What Remains*. He is based in Kinshasa.

Jaan Kaplinski is an Estonian poet, philosopher and translator. A critic of the Soviet regime, after its collapse he served as a member of the Estonian Parliament. In 2014 he released his first collection of poems written in Russian, *White Butterflies of Night*.

Megan McDowell translates from the Spanish. Her translations of Alejandro Zambra have appeared in several publications, including the *New Yorker*, *Harper's*, *Words Without Borders* and the *Paris Review*. She lives in Santiago.

Lorenzo Meloni is an Italian photographer. His work has been published in *L'Espresso* and *TIME*.

Claire Messud is the author of *The Emperor's Children*, shortlisted for the 2006 Man Booker Prize. Her other works include *The Last Life*, *When the World Was Steady* and *The Hunters*. Her most recent novel is *The Woman Upstairs*.

Herta Müller is the winner of the 2009 Nobel Prize in Literature. Her books include *The Hunger Angel*, *The Appointment* and *The Land of Green Plums*. Born in Romania in 1953, Müller emigrated to Berlin in 1987, where she now lives. 'The Way of the Apple Worm' is taken from *The Fox Was Ever the Hunter*, forthcoming from Metropolitan Books and Portobello Books in 2016.

Philip Ó Ceallaigh is an Irish author and translator. His translation of Mihail Sebastian's *For Two Thousand Years* is forthcoming from Penguin in 2016. 'Bucharest, Broken City' is taken from a work in progress on Eastern Europe, the Holocaust and totalitarianism.

Peter Pomerantsev is a Kiev-born writer and TV producer living in London. He is the author of *Nothing Is True and Everything Is Possible*, an account of contemporary life inside Putin's dictatorship. His writing has appeared in several publications, including the *London Review of Books*, the *Atlantic* and *Newsweek*.

Eric Puchner is the author of the story collection *Music Through the Floor* and the novel *Model Home*. His work has appeared in *GQ*, *Tin House*, *Zoetrope* and *The Best American Short Stories*. He teaches at Johns Hopkins University.

David Rakoff (1964–2012) is the author of the essay collections *Fraud*, *Don't Get Too Comfortable* and *Half Empty*, and the novel *Love, Dishonor, Marry, Die, Cherish, Perish*. His writing frequently appeared in the *New York Times*, *Newsweek*, *Wired*, *Salon*, *GQ*, *Outside*, *Gourmet*, *Vogue* and *Slate*.

Solmaz Sharif's work has appeared in the *New Republic* and *Poetry*. Her first poetry collection, *Look*, is published by Graywolf Press in July 2016. She is a Jones Lecturer at Stanford University.

Matthew Welton's third collection, *The Number Poems* will be published by Carcanet in 2016. He teaches creative writing at the University of Nottingham.

Alejandro Zambra is the author of two poetry collections, a book of essays and three novels, including *Ways of Going Home*. He was one of *Granta*'s Best of Young Spanish Language Novelists in 2010. He lives in Santiago and is a literature professor at Diego Portales University. 'Reading Comprehension: Text No. 2' is taken from *Multiple Choice*, forthcoming from Granta Books in the UK and Penguin Books in the US in 2016.

Same magazine, different format

New app out now

GRANTA.COM

GRANTA

THE MAGAZINE OF NEW WRITING

PRINT SUBSCRIPTION REPLY FORM FOR US, CANADA
AND LATIN AMERICA (includes digital and app access).
For digital-only subscriptions, please visit granta.com/subscriptions.

GUARANTEE: If I am ever dissatisfied with my *Granta* subscription, I will simply notify you, and you will send me a complete refund or credit my credit card, as applicable, for all un-mailed issues.

YOUR DETAILS

TITLE ....

NAME ....

ADDRESS ....

....

CITY.. STATE ....

ZIP CODE .... COUNTRY...............................

EMAIL ....

☐ Please check this box if you do not wish to receive special offers from *Granta*
☐ Please check this box if you do not wish to receive offers from organisations selected by *Granta*

PAYMENT DETAILS

1 year subscription: ☐ US: $48 ☐ Canada: $56 ☐ Latin America: $68

3 year subscription: ☐ US: $120 ☐ Canada: $144 ☐ Latin America: $180

Enclosed is my check for $ ⎯⎯⎯⎯⎯ made payable to *Granta*.

Please charge my: ☐ Visa ☐ MasterCard ☐ Amex

Card No. ☐☐☐☐☐☐☐☐☐☐☐☐☐☐☐☐

Expiration date ☐☐ / ☐☐

Security Code [⎯⎯⎯⎯]

SIGNATURE .... DATE ....

Please mail this order form with your payment instructions to:

Granta Publications
PO Box 359
Congers, NY 10920-0359

Or call 845-267-3031
Or visit GRANTA.COM/SUBSCRIPTIONS for details

Source code: BUS134PM